HOME HANDYMAN
PLUMBING AND DRAINAGE

AURA
BOOKS

CONTENTS

Editor: Mary Lambert
Designer: Eljay Crompton

This edition published by
Aura Book Distribution Limited
2 Derby Road, Greenford, Middlesex

Produced by
Marshall Cavendish Books Limited
58 Old Compton Street, London W1V 5PA

© Marshall Cavendish Limited 1984
ISBN 0 86307 261 5
Printed and bound in Milan, Italy by New Interlitho

Plumbing and Drainage gives you all the know-how you need to carry out a range of basic jobs like plumbing in a washing machine or installing a shower. There's also information on how to deal with hard water and airlocks, plus advice on what to do when a tap starts to drip or a pipe bursts unexpectedly

Understanding your water system

Domestic water systems come in two main types:

High-pressure systems, in which water at 'mains pressure' is supplied directly to all the taps and other water-using appliances.

Low-pressure systems, in which the water supply to most taps and appliances is via a cold-water storage cistern in the attic, only the kitchen tap(s) being supplied directly from the mains.

This section deals with low-pressure systems, which are common in the UK.

Where the water comes from

Cold water comes to your house from the water authority mains via a smaller, service pipe. This pipe may have been installed specifically to serve your house or you many share it with a neighbour. Either way, it will be controlled by a water authority stopcock somewhere on the edge of your, or your neighbour's, property. The stopcock is sunk below ground (usually about a metre) and is encased in brickwork, concrete, or a stoneware pipe to provide access. To mark the site, a small cast-iron casing is usually fitted at ground level.

From here, the service pipe runs to your house and becomes known as the rising main. At the point where it enters, a further stopcock—known as the consumer's, or house, stopcock—is fitted. This one is your own personal property and, because it controls all the water entering the house, it is as well to know exactly where you can locate it.

The most common place is under the kitchen sink, where a branch of the rising main directly supplies the kitchen cold tap with drinking water. The other most likely locations are under the stairs, or maybe situated below the floorboards immediately inside the front door.

	Hot water feed to radiators
	Cooled water return from radiators
	Cooled water from heat exchanger
	Hot water feed to heat exchanger
	Rising supply main (cold)
	Cold supply from storage cistern
	Hot water supply from cylinder

Left: A typical modern plumbing system incorporates two hot water loops for the hot water cylinder and radiators. The water enters the house via the rising main and then feeds the heating system from the supply tank

3

The cold storage tank

After the branch to the kitchen cold tap, the rising main runs to a cold storage tank or cistern, normally in the roof space. Older storage tanks are made of galvanized iron, which is both heavy and prone to rust. These have now been replaced by the lighter, more hygienic, plastic tanks.

The storage tank helps to iron out irregularities in the mains supply and also provides an emergency reservoir if the supply is cut off.

The rising main's supply of water to the top of the tank is controlled by a ball-valve similar to the one in a WC cistern. At the base of the storage tank you will find the main water outlet. The stored water flows through here under the pressure of gravity and then branches off to supply the rest of your house's water requirements. These will include the WC, the bathroom cold taps and the hot water cylinder.

A stopcock is normally fitted somewhere near the outlet, so that you can turn off most of the water but still leave your kitchen cold tap in operation to supply the family's needs while you are working.

The hot water supply

In household plumbing, cold water is converted to hot either directly or indirectly. Direct heating means that the cold water comes into direct contact with a heater—normally a boiler or an electric immersion heater—then flows straight to the taps.

With indirect heating—usually combined with central heating—the water heated by the boiler is itself used to heat up fresh cold water. In this system, the two hot water circuits are separate and heat is transferred from one to the other by means of a heat exchanger.

The hot water cylinder, a copper tank heavily insulated to guard against heat loss, is common to most hot water installations.

In direct systems, it houses the electric immersion heaters—if fitted—and acts as a storage tank to keep your hot water supply as constant as possible. In an indirect system, the cylinder has the additional function of housing the heat exchanger.

The direct flow

The flow of water in both direct and indirect systems relies on the principle that hot water always rises above the cold water around it. So, in a direct system, the flow starts with cold water running to the base of the hot water cylinder.

If a boiler is fitted then the flow continues from the cylinder down to the base of the boiler. As the water is heated it rises out through the top of the boiler, up to the top of the hot water cylinder and then on to the hot taps.

If immersion heaters are fitted instead of a boiler, the flow is greatly simplified. The water runs from the storage tank to the base of the hot water cylinder and is heated: it then rises straight out of the cylinder and on to the hot taps.

The great disadvantage of direct systems is that water, when it is heated above 60°C (140°F)—or 80°C (176°F) in soft water areas—deposits scale similar to kettle fur.

The scale can block up pipework and boilers alike unless adequate precautions are taken. These include keeping the water temperature down below the 'scaling point' and using scale-inhibiting additives in your cold storage tank.

The indirect flow

The easiest way of understanding an indirect hot water flow is to visualize two independent 'loops' of water. The first loop consists of the water used to feed the hot taps.

This flows from the cold storage tank to the base of the hot water cylinder, where it comes into thermal contact with hot water on the other loop (via the heat exchanger). As the water is heated, it rises out of the cylinder and on to supply the taps.

The other loop supplies the boiler, heat

exchanger and—if fitted—the radiators. Here, fresh water flows to the base of the boiler from either the storage tank or from another separate tank, which is known as the 'expansion tank'.

Once in the boiler, the water is heated and then rises out to feed the heat exchanger and radiators. After the water has given up its heat, it flows directly back to the boiler again for re-heating.

Because the water in this loop is hardly ever changed, the problems of scaling are greatly reduced. The first time it is heated, the water gives up its scale; from then on, it is unable to do further damage.

The expansion tank

The indirect arrangement works best when an expansion tank is fitted to supply the boiler loop. This makes the loop almost completely independent of the one supplying the hot taps.

The tank is supplied with water from the rising main via another ball-valve. So, if the loop needs topping up with water because of evaporation, the process is automatic. In practice, however, you will find changes in the water level inside the expansion tank are barely noticeable.

To guard against the build-up of high pressures in the hot water system, safety overflows or vents are fitted.

In a direct system, only one pipe is needed. This runs to the top of the cold storage tank, either from the crown of the hot water cylinder or from a branch which is off the hot water service pipe.

In an indirect system, an additional vent is installed at the top point of the primary circuit.

Turning off the hot water

Whatever your hot water system, the hot water which reaches the taps comes from the top of your hot water cylinder. It does so because of the pressure of the cold water entering the cylinder beneath.

So, if you cut off the cold water supply at the base of the cylinder, no further hot water will rise from the top. Most hot water cylinders have a stopcock for this purpose, fitted at the cold water inlet. Those that do not, invariably have a stopcock somewhere on the pipe between the inlet and the cold storage tank. Before touching this stopcock make sure that all heating apparatus is turned off.

Wet central heating

Wet central heating, in which hot water is used to heat the house via a system of radiators, adds an additional complication to plumbing installations. But if you can imagine the radiators and their pipes as being part of the boiler 'loop' in a basic hot water system, the whole thing becomes easier to understand.

Some older installations work on the direct principle in which hot water heated by the boiler flows to the radiators as well as to the hot taps. Because this system is uneconomical and causes scaling, it has been replaced by indirect installations.

Here, the water which flows to the radiators is on a pump-driven loop like the one used to supply the heat exchanger. Consequently it is always fairly hot and requires less heating, which in turn makes it far more economical and efficient than a direct system.

In some indirect systems, the water which supplies the boiler loop is drawn direct from the storage tank. But most incorporate a separate expansion tank to keep the loop independent of the rest of the water supply.

Radiator systems

The pipework used to supply the radiators may take one of two forms. In the simpler, one-pipe system, hot water flows from the boiler to each radiator in turn and then back to the boiler again. Although this cuts down the amount of pipework needed, it allows hot and cooled water to mix near the end of the run. Consequently, the last radiator in the run often remains rather cool however hard the boiler itself is working.

In the two-pipe system, the pipework is

5

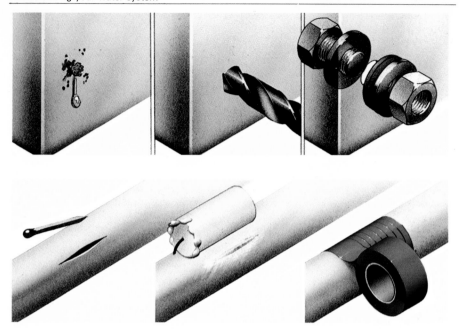

Above: If you are unlucky enough to have a leak or burst pipe, your first step must be to cut off the water supply. Do this as near to the damage as possible so that inconvenience is minimal. When it is a hot water pipe or tap look for a stopcock on the pipe which runs into the base of the hot water cylinder or boiler. Before you turn it, make sure that all heating apparatus is off. With a cold water pipe or tap you should trace back along the pipe until you come to a stopcock. If there is none between the burst and the cold storage tank you will have to block the tank outlet. To do this, nail a cork slightly larger than the outlet hole to a piece of timber. By feel, you can now insert the cork into the outlet to block it. A leak in the tank (top) can often be fixed by plugging the hole with a bolt. Use a soft washer between the two metal rings for a close fit. Temporary repairs (bottom) can be made to a split lead pipe by plugging the crack with a bit of matchstick, waxing the plug, then taping it together firmly

arranged so that cooled water leaving the radiators cannot mix with the hot water entering them. The radiators therefore heat up faster, as well as remaining at the same temperature.

Sizing of inward and outward piping in the radiator circuit is matched to the given radiator load—so pipe sizes can vary quite a lot throughout the different systems.

Water is forced around the circuit by means of an electrically driven pump, placed either in the flow or return pipe, close to, or in, the boiler.

Even without the use of a pump, water can flow around the circuit by natural circulation—this method of gravity flow is widely used for heating domestic hot water. It is rarely used for central heating because it requires large-diameter pipes with relatively short and simple pipe runs. Even so, most central heating systems will circulate by gravity to some extent when the pump is switched off, unless a control valve has been fitted to the system.

Controlling the water flow

In any domestic water system the flow of water through the pipes can be carefully regulated by taps, shut-off valves and stopcocks. When closed any of these devices should shut off the flow completely—and when open they should not obstruct the flow at all. Inefficient or damaged taps can lead to problems and leaks elsewhere in the system. And a leaky tap in the hot water circuit can be costly, letting expensively heated water dribble away. So a smooth uninterrupted flow of water is essential and can only be guaranteed by the correct choice and placement of fittings.

Three parts of the domestic system have an important bearing on the flow of water through the pipes. The main stopcock or valve controls the flow of water into the system from the outside water supply. As it proceeds around the pipes, the water flow is regulated by a number of subsidiary valves.

Turning a stopcock

Probably the most important fitting in any domestic system is the mains stopcock, since it is this that allows water to enter the system from the outside supply. If you are unlucky enough to have a leak or want to carry out major repairs to the system, the water must be turned off at this stopcock before work can begin.

Make sure you know exactly where this stopcock is located—otherwise a sudden leak will find you unprepared. In the UK it is usually to be found under a key-hole-shaped metal cover near the front boundary of the house.

When the cover is open the stopcock handle should be visible about 600mm (in the UK) below ground level. Quite often it

is covered in soil; clear this away by hand, or with a stick if the hole is too narrow.

If you cannot reach the handle, use a turning key to grasp the stopcock. Make a key by cutting a wide V-shaped notch from the bottom of a long piece of waste wood (fig. 5).

Many main stopcocks do not have a cross-head handle like a tap, but are fitted with a four-sided shank, over which a special turnkey must be fitted to operate the valve. The local water authority needs to be contacted before the supply is turned off as they can supply the key.

Many modern houses have a second stopcock or valve situated just inside the house, and cutting off the water at this point is usually far easier. Look for this stopcock under the kitchen sink.

Relining a stopcock

The drain recess surrounding a mains stopcock is usually strong enough to last for some time, but often it becomes damaged by ground movement—or pressure from the paving stones above—and the pipe surrounding the drain splits. When this occurs a new stopcock pit needs to be constructed in its place.

A 150mm diameter stoneware pipe should be cut to length to make the new liner and placed with the belled end uppermost, to enable a new lid to be fitted on top.

Fitting valves

If you want to carry out repair work on a small part of the water system it is very disruptive to turn off the whole supply at the main. This means that all of the water

1 To turn the mains stopcock, find the key-hole-shaped cover—it is usually on the edge of your property

2 If the cover has become jammed or is at all difficult to raise, bend a piece of wire and insert it into the drain hole

3 Use the wire to lever the cover upwards and over to one side to expose the drain and the stopcock

4 Often the stopcock handle is covered with dirt and needs to be cleared before turning with a piece of stick

5 Many drains are too narrow to accommodate your hand, so cut a 'V' shape out of a spare piece of wood

6 The notch can then be fitted comfortably around the tap handle and the stopcock turned gently on or off

system is out of action while the work is being done.

It is far easier to install valves at various points which can be used to isolate particular sections of pipework. There are two types of valves which are in general use—*gate valves* and *isolating valves*. To be effective great care must be taken in positioning them correctly.

Gate valves: These usually have wheel-type handles and are fitted within lengths of pipework. Their main use is in UK cistern-fed supplies, where they are fitted in pipes leading out from the cold water cistern—either to the hot water cylinder, or to cold taps (usually just those upstairs) and for fittings such as WCs.

When fitting gate valves, position them where they are clearly visible and can be reached in an emergency. The best places are in the airing cupboard for the supply to the hot water tank and on the outlet from the cold water cistern in the loft for the supply to the cold taps.

Special care needs to be taken when

cutting off the supply to the hot water tank. Once the valve is shut off water is prevented from entering the tank and so the immersion heater should immediately be switched off.

Isolating valves: These are neat inline fittings used to isolate individual sections of pipework. They can usefully be employed to shut off the water supply to items such as water heaters or taps.

Using draincocks
One of the simplest types of taps is the draincock which is' used throughout central heating systems but also has many applications in the domestic water system. It is used to drain difficult sections of pipe.

Draincocks can be fitted to almost any length of pipework, but in most domestic water systems they are used to drain the hot water tank or the rising main. Before emptying any of these parts of the system the appropriate gate valve needs to be closed off first.

Do remember to check with your local water authority, or with your local plumbing codes, as to whether or not you need approval before starting *any* plumbing work.

A. Below: To reline a stopcock pit cut a 150mm diameter stoneware pipe to length using a hammer and bolster. Then chip out two U-shaped slots to fit around underground pipes. Turn over, fill with sand and line the bell with brown paper. Then cast a concrete lid which has a wire handle

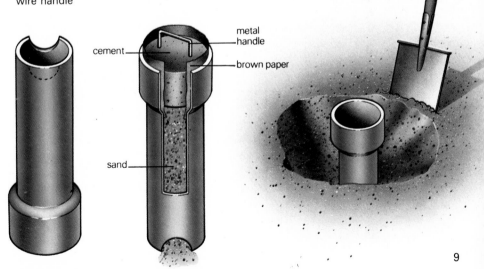

cement

metal handle

brown paper

sand

9

Types of taps

Fitting plain and mixer taps is a relatively simple operation if it is tackled with care. What is far more difficult is to choose the type of tap which is suitable for your needs. Practical considerations such as clear marking of hot and cold and ease of movement when turning on and off are as important as how the tap looks.

Pillar tap: This is the most popular type of tap widely used for basins and baths. It has a vertical inlet and is available in two sizes. The 15mm variety is normally fitted to sinks and wash basins while the 22mm type is more suitable for baths or extra large sinks.

Bib taps: This type of tap has a horizontal inlet and in most homes it is used to provide water for the garage or garden. Ideally it is fitted with a threaded nozzle so that a hose connector can be screwed on. Usually a bib tap is secured to an outside wall and a plate elbow needs to be used.

Supataps: These are UK taps, unlike others both in appearance and operation. Most have handles with plastic ears which do not conduct heat and are easy to grip. But their main distinctive feature is that the handle is part of the spout outlet and turns with the tap. Because of their construction Supataps can be re-washered without turning off the water supply.

Mixer taps

Mixer taps differ from plain taps—they still have two inlets but instead of having separate hot and cold taps, both are combined in one outlet.

Sink mixers: These type of taps have nozzles which contain two separate waterways—one for the hot supply and the other for cold water. It is built in this complicated way to accommodate regulations which do not allow cold water from the main to mix with hot water which has come from a storage tank. This is to avoid the risk of mains water becoming contaminated by coming into contact with the stored water.

Because of this divided flow system these type of mixers are often uncomfortable to wash your hands under—one part gets scalded, the other frozen.

In the UK, where the hot water also comes direct from the mains (via an

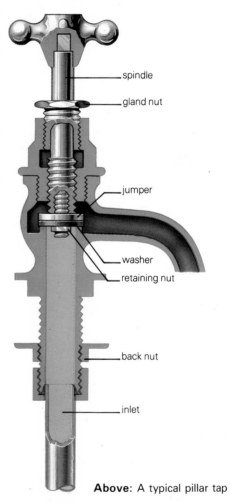

spindle

gland nut

jumper

washer

retaining nut

back nut

inlet

Above: A typical pillar tap

Above: This mixer tap has plastic handwheels which match the bath. It is also fitted with an outlet and automatic instantaneous water heater for example), divided flow mixers are not necessary.

diverter on the spout to which it is very easy to fit a modern shower attachment

Bath mixers: The type of mixer usually referred to by this name does not work on the divided flow principle but mixes the two water flows inside the taps themselves. These are usually permitted even in the UK, because both hot and cold water in a bathroom usually come via the cistern. But they are not allowed in areas where all the cold water is direct from the mains (unless the hot water also comes direct from the mains—again perhaps via an instantaneous heater). Check with your local water authority if in doubt.

Special tap attachments
There is a whole range of fittings which can be bought as attachments to taps which make them more attractive and practical.

Swivel nozzles: Many taps, particularly the mixer type can be fitted with swivelling nozzles. These move from side to side and enable the flow of water to be directed to feed both sides of a unit which is fitted with two sinks or bowls.

Shower attachments: These are normally fitted to mixer taps over baths. A separate switch usually mounted on top of the tap allows you to divert the water to the shower head which can be positioned on a rail above the bath.

Above: Some types of tap are fitted with both vertical and horizontal inlet fittings

11

Dealing with hard water

Water supplied for domestic use is purified to make it bacteria-free—and therefore fit for human consumption—by efficient filtration and storage, as well as by additives and treatments introduced by the water authorities. But even this water contains impurities, in the form of certain amounts of dissolved mineral salts that are referred to when we talk of the *hardness* or *softness* of water.

What is hard water?
Rainwater which falls in open country and on to insoluble rock such as slate or granite remains more or less mineral-free. Surface water may, however, pick up organic waste products. This water is usually *soft*.

Conversely, rainwater which falls on to sedimentary rocks tends to permeate through these to emerge as ground water which has a high dissolved mineral content. This water is relatively *hard*.

But there is another side to consider. As rainwater falls to earth it picks up quantities of gases and pollutants which acidify it slightly. The most significant of these acids generally is carbonic acid (soda water), produced by the solution of atmospheric carbon dioxide; but in heavily industrialized areas, with a far greater proportion of sulphur dioxide, rain can actually fall as a very dilute form of sulphuric acid.

The mildly acid rainwater falls on, and is absorbed by, different rock strata, during which time it reacts with minerals in the rocks themselves. It then either disgorges into rivers, lakes and reservoirs or collects underground and is pumped to the surface.

In regions where there is a high pro-portion of calcium and magnesium carbonate in the rock—found in limestone and chalky soil, and dolomites respectively—the carbonic acid in the rainwater reacts with the carbonates to produce bicarbonates.

It is these that make the water obviously 'hard' and pose the greatest threat to domestic water systems. At low temperatures, the bicarbonates are readily soluble in water and remain so until they reach your system. But when this water is heated, they begin to decompose into insoluble carbonates which are deposited on any surface at a temperature past the critical point.

The problem of scale and scum
Scale is the build-up of particles of the bicarbonates released from hard water when it is heated. This precipitation begins at around 60°C (140°F) and accelerates as the temperature is raised. It is for this reason that the first signs of scale are usually found in the kettle.

Much more serious is the effect of scale on hot water pipes and central heating systems: pipes become clogged, valves and pumps can jam, and boiler efficiency and life may be drastically reduced.

Testing your water
The hardness of water varies considerably. If the water is very hard, kettle furring and scummy baths are a clear sign. But if your soap lathers easily and the water feels soft to the touch, you have soft water.

Your water supply authority should be able to tell you a great deal about the water you receive, and may be able to test any water that comes into your home.

Low cost, easy-to-use *water hardness test kits* are readily available from aquarist supply shops. These employ indicator chemicals and you simply count the number of drops needed to effect a colour change in order to obtain a very accurate hardness reading.

Treatments of hard water

A number of possible options exist for the treatment of hard water. Some merely condition it, others actually soften it. The latest development is specifically intended to combat the scale caused by heating.

Chemical scale inhibitors do not actually soften water, but instead stabilize the bicarbonates so that they do not form carbonate scale. You need an indirect low-pressure plumbing system—a plastic container of crystals is suspended inside the cold water cistern.

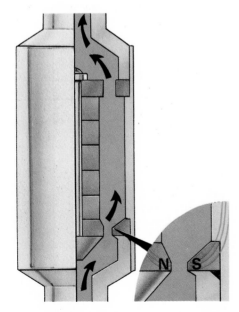

A. Above: In a magnetic conditioner, the water flows through a magnetic field. This affects the particles in the water and helps to reduce the scale

This method is cheap but the crystals do need replacing.

The same principle is applied in *descaling units*—small containers of crystals which are actually plumbed into the rising main piping. Versions of this device are available for use with chemicals specifically intended to counteract water containing too much iron or acid.

Most recent of the developments is the *magnetic conditioner* which does not actually change any of the chemical properties of the water, and therefore does not influence its taste and nutritional properties. The conditioner works by passing the water close to strong magnets. These are thought to alter the magnetic properties of the micro-particles enough to dissuade both scale and scum from forming.

Conditioners do not actually soften the water—for this you need a proper *water softener*. These work by actually removing bicarbonate salts from the water in a process known as ion exchange.

Very simply, ion exchange in a water softener takes place when the electrically-charged bicarbonate ions in the water pass over a catalyst known as the *resin bed*. Here, they change places with ions of sodium and thereafter remain attached to the resin bed while the sodium ions pass harmlessly into the water.

Eventually the resin attracts enough bicarbonate ions to become clogged and it must then be flushed clear with brine solution—which is powerful enough to overwhelm and displace the bicarbonate ions. In all makes of modern water softener this recharging takes place automatically, using salt from a built-in reservoir.

Installing a water softener

The best place to install a water softener is in a kitchen or laundry room—or wherever the rising main first emerges.

You usually need permission before doing plumbing work—check with your local authority or plumbing codes.

Specific instructions vary from make to make, but generally the work entails interrupting the rising main at a convenient point above the main stopcock and then installing inlet and outlet pipes to the softener—the latter rejoining the old rising main to restore a supply link. Between the inlet and outlet pipes, a bypass valve can be located to disconnect the softener for regular maintenance work.

Both the inlet and the outlet pipes are usually provided with shut-off valves. But check with your water authorities to see if they require the inclusion of a non-return/air-brake valve. If so, this is located between the inlet valve and the softener.

In areas with particularly high water pressure, you must guard against this exceeding the capabilities of the softener by fitting a pressure reducer between the mains stopcock and the inlet pipe junction.

Drain and overflow pipework usually take the form of hosepipes. The drain is often led to a standpipe arrangement incorporating a P-trap, based on the same principle as the drain pipework for a washing machine. The overflow pipe is led independently to the outside.

Ideally, cut the pipework to individual lengths and lay these in a dry run with fittings loosely arranged to check the plumbing-in arrangement before final assembly. Compression or capillary fittings can be used for the inlet and outlet connections to the rising main, though the latter are considerably cheaper.

Follow specific recommendations for making the electrical connections. Although most units can be connected via a fused plug to an ordinary switched socket, it is better to wire the unit to a fused spur or connection box to prevent water getting into contact with live wires and causing an accident.

After electrical connection, all that remains is to programme and start up the unit—following the manufacturer's specific instructions.

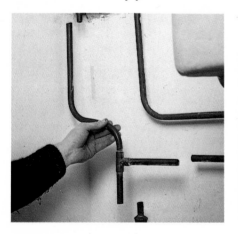

1 Before installing the new pipework for a water softener, close off the main stopcock to completely shut off the water supply and drain it down. The new pipework is inserted into the rising main at a convenient point above the main stopcock. Also cut away the old pipework at this point in the operation

2 A great deal of care should be taken when working with all forms of pipework. When joining sections of pipework, always try to remember to smear a little jointing compound around the faces of the joints. This will really help to ensure the necessary watertight seal needed when the system is working

3 When all your joints are thoroughly smeared with jointing compound, the new pipe and valve assembly, that you are constructing, should then be built up section by section. Then it should be carefully connected up, via the non-return valve, to the hard water inlet which is already in existence

4 Make sure that the cut inlet pipe is then capped off. If a separate hard water supply is required, the pipe may be connected later. In this particular type of installation, water flows to a washing machine through a completely separate pipe. This is then connected to the assembly last

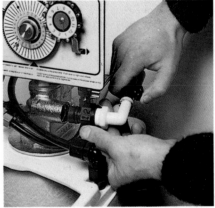

5 Once the assembly is in place, make sure that all three valves are closed off, then turn the stopcock back on to renew the normal water supply. Waste water flows from this softener through an overflow and a drain hose. Arrange for these to discharge out at a suitable drainage point for your chosen location

6 With the softener fitted in its correct location, secure the hoses running from it to the overflow and drain with plastic hose clips. Connect the drainage hose to the drainage outlet which is situated below the control mechanism, then firmly connect up the required overflow hose section

7 The two hoses which run from the softener to the pipe and valve assembly are joined to the machine by plastic nipple attachments. Once these nipples are firmly in place, connect up the hoses. The hard water inlet is situated at the top, with the soft water outlet featured below

8 Connect up the hose running from the inlet on the machine to the inlet valve and the hose from the outlet to the outlet valve above it. Then, next, having turned off the electricity supply at the main fuse box, wire a suitable amount of electric cable from the softener control valve to a fused spur

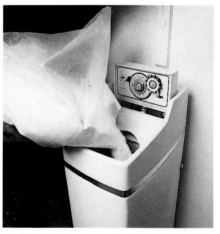

9 With the wiring connected, fix the old switch and the cover of the fused spur in place but do not turn on the power at this stage. Then follow the instructions for manual regeneration to flush out the cylinder. Initial dirty water will flow to the drain

10 Replace the top cover assembly of the softener, then pour granular salt into the filling hole at the top of the machine. With the valves open, the unit programmed and the power turned on, the new softener is ready to be fully tested in operation

Plumbing with plastics

Plastic pipe is rapidly taking the place of more traditional forms of pipework in many areas of plumbing. Of the reasons why this is so, the most obvious is that plastics is an easy material to work with. But most forms are also immune to chemical attack from the ground on which they are laid and the water which they carry. And plastic piping is comparatively inexpensive and versatile in its application.

However, most forms of plastic distort when heated, so plastic plumbing pipe is usually used only for waste systems which rarely carry hot water for long, or for cold water supplies.

Note: Before carrying out any work, check your proposals with the appropriate authorities.

Plastics used in plumbing

The plastic most commonly used is PVC (polyvinyl chloride) available for plumbing uses in both unplasticized (uPVC or rigid vinyl) and in post-chlorinated forms (cPVC). Without added plasticizer, PVC is an extremely hard and rigid material. But because additional compounds such as plasticizers and hardeners can be added to it, in the process changing some of its properties, it is essential to specify exactly what you want it for when ordering materials.

Like all the plastics used for pipes, PVC is a thermoplastic. This means that it softens and then melts on heating, but unlike some plastics PVC will not support combustion. In addition, PVC is light but not weak, and rigid without being too brittle and is used for low-pressure plumbing applications.

Here, PVC is used for a wide variety of pipework including that for rainwater, soil, waste, below-ground drainage and some cold water services.

ABS (acrylonitrile butadiene styrene) is commonly used for fittings and some waste runs of normal diameters, but not usually for soil installations in the UK.

Polyethylene or polythene is perhaps the most widespread of all plastics materials, but its use in plumbing is confined mainly to fittings. In its high density form it is a tough material and one which can be used for liquids up to 100°C (212°F) but like its derivative, polypropylene, it has the disadvantage of melting and burning like paraffin wax when heated by a naked flame.

Polypropylene has a significantly higher softening point and can manage steam and liquids up to a temperature of 100°C (212°F).

These two materials, generically termed polyolefins, are used for stable-temperature cold water supplies and for drainage where there is low risk of hot waste. Another popular use is for running a water supply into the garden.

Nylon has a much better resistance to higher temperature than most other thermoplastics and is sometimes considered suitable for pressure installations—in central heating systems it can manage temperatures of between 80°C and 120°C (176°F and 248°F).

Telling the plastics apart

As this is important, not only to avoid fitting the wrong material but also to make use of the most satisfactory method of jointing, shave off a small sliver from the test pipe and see how this responds to the flame of a match when held carefully in metal tweezers. PVC will be self-extinguishing when removed from the flame, whereas ABS and nylon will continue to burn—the nylon albeit reluctantly and smelling like burnt hair.

Methods of joining plastic pipe

Two forms of joint are used for joining

17

together lengths of plastic pipe in the same material: the ring sealed joint and the solvent welded joint.

Ring sealed joint

This is a push-fit, semi-permanent connection, axially rigid enough for normal use, but capable of absorbing lengthways expansion. This and easy assembly explain the joint's widespread popularity.

In one half of the joint a synthetic rubber ring is housed near the mouth of the socket at the end of the pipe. The introduction of a spigot—the plain but chamfered end of the other pipe—compresses the ring within its recess to provide a firm seal which can be forced apart if and when required.

Where possible, pipes are joined with the flow in a socket-to-spigot direction to minimize the effect of the spigot if the edge of this is not fully home against the socket.

The pipe around the ring seal joint is at least as strong as a plain section of pipe and is quite capable of withstanding the same amount of pressure. This and its characteristic flexibility make it useful for most underground mains supplies and any drains.

The solvent welded joint

Also known as the solvent cement joint, this can be used for all the usual applications of PVC and ABS plastics, and is a particular favourite for the latter. Because it is a permanent joint, which cannot be accidentally knocked apart, it is usually the first choice also for water supply systems.

Unlike ring seal joints, which on underground bends and on pipework exposed to accidental knocking or external pressure must be supported on either side, solvent welded joints need no protective support.

Solvent joints cannot, however, be used with the polyolefins or nylon and a further disadvantage is that expansion joints—ring seal joints—must still be included in straight sections.

Bending plastic pipe

Although most of the plastics are elastic to some degree, only polythene is considered 'bendable' by plumbing standards. In this a temporary bend can be formed by suitably positioned pipe fixings. A permanent bend is made by heating the bend section for about ten minutes in boiling water, then bending it to the required degree and leaving it to cool in this shape.

Making a ring seal joint

To prepare the spigot end, cut the pipe end perfectly square using a fine-toothed saw—a large hacksaw with 32 teeth per 25mm is ideal. If the pipe end is not square it may strike the ring seal at an awkward angle and displace it during the course of assembly. A straight cut is not difficult on small-bore tube, but some form of template or guide is a useful aid on thicker pipe.

A quick method is to wrap a sheet of straight-edged paper around the pipe and to use the matched up edge of this as a cutting guide (fig. 5). But if you are doing much work, it is more convenient in the long run to make a template from an offcut of pipe socket. Cut a small section from this so that you form a 'C'-shape then clip it over the pipe and use its edge as a guide (fig. 1).

After you have cut the pipe end remove the internal and external burr, using a rasp for PVC and ABS and a sharp knife for polyolefins.

You then chamfer the outer edge of the pipe to enable the spigot to be easily inserted in the socket and compress the ring seal. Chamfering is especially important on larger diameter pipe and is done for both ring seal and solvent joints. A shaping tool—such as a Surform—can be used to produce a chamfer on ABS or PVC, but a special tool is required for polypropylene and this is usually supplied by the manufacturer of the pipe.

A guide line marked no less than 5mm from the pipe end helps to ensure an even, shallow-sloped (15°) bevel around the edge.

1 Use a fine-toothed hacksaw to cut plastics pipe. Make a 'C'-shaped cutting guide from an offcut to ensure that the cuts are straight

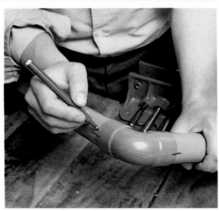

2 Dry assemble a solvent joint and make alignment marks for direction and depth as there is no other way of checking the assembly later

3 Clean all traces of dirt and grease from the contact areas of the spigot and socket. Then apply solvent cement to the cleaned contact areas

4 Immediately afterwards, push the spigot into the socket and hold the assembly firmly for 15 seconds. Then remove all the excess solvent

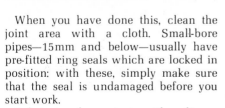

When you have done this, clean the joint area with a cloth. Small-bore pipes—15mm and below—usually have pre-fitted ring seals which are locked in position: with these, simply make sure that the seal is undamaged before you start work.

Lubricate the spigot with silicone grease just before inserting it. Do not use soap or detergent as this may become solidified near the ring seal.

A slight twisting and screwing motion makes inserting the spigot easier. Push it nearly home but leave an expansion gap between the stop of the fitting and the end of the pipe.

Special jointing clamps may have to be used for ring-seal (and solvent) joints made in pipe which is 200mm diameter and over.

Making a solvent joint

A solvent joint is normally made only in pipes and fittings of the same material and care must be taken in matching new materials to any existing pipework. However, there is a variety of adaptors that allow connection of different materials, for example uPVC to cast-iron.

The preparation stages for a solvent joint are the same as for a ring seal joint. After chamfering the spigot, remove any dust or dirt from the pipe fitting with a dry cloth then assemble the pipes and fittings in a dry run to determine the best work order. It is important that all minor problems are sorted out at this stage. Insert the spigot fully home and mark the pipe at the socket edge when it is so. During later assembly this is the only sign that assembly is correct.

Next, apply a proprietary cleaning fluid or methylated spirits to the contact area using a dry cloth. This acts as a degreasing agent and in the process removes the glossy surface of the pipe. The contact area must remain free of dirt and grease thereafter, so handle the pipe carefully during any dry run checks. On 'smooth' smaller-bore pipe, dislodged abrasive particles can become embedded in the surface of the contact area and affect the efficiency of the joint. Be especially cautious over the use of emery paper, and under no circumstances use steel wool for this job.

Immediately after cleaning, apply an even layer of solvent cement to the prepared contact area with a clean, flat brush—or a spatula in the case of thick cement. Take care not to use too much. *Note:* Solvent cement and cleaning fluid are highly volatile and should be used only in a well-ventilated room.

Push the pipe and fitting together with a slight twisting motion and hold the assembly—under pressure—for about 15 seconds, then immediately remove excess solvent with a dry cloth. Do not disturb the joint for a further two minutes. A full strength bond is achieved after several hours, but it is advisable to wait a day before using.

It is good practice and more convenient to assemble a section of pipework with dry fittings and then solvent weld several at a time. Use a pencil and rule to check alignment as each solvent weld is made.

Test pipe joins before a final connection to an existing run if you can. Fill the new run with water and leave it to stand, checking for leaks later.

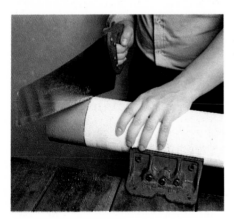

5 Use an old handsaw to cut large diameter pipe. A cutting guide can then be made by lining up the edges of a loop of paper

6 Roughen up the surface of large diameter pipe using a glasspaper pad. Never be tempted to use steel wool for this job—it is just too harsh

Protecting your pipework

Most substances expand when they are heated and contract as they cool. But water expands when it freezes, and this unusual property makes every part of the domestic water system a potential disaster area in a frost.

The effects of a freeze-up

Ice forming in a water supply system can have two very harmful effects. The pressure that it exerts as it expands can cause pipes to split or joints to come adrift, and it can also block vital sections of pipe so that parts of the house receive no water.

Often, the worst damage occurs when the ice in frozen pipework melts. Water leaking from cracked pipes or damaged joints can ruin decorations and make dangerous contact with electrical equipment.

Boiler explosions and cylinder implosions are, thankfully, much rarer; but both could occur during very cold weather when the house has either been left empty for a while, or allowed to cool abnormally overnight.

Most UK hot water systems operate through the circulation of water under pressure from the cold water cistern, and for this reason an expansion vent pipe is fitted between the cistern and the hot water cylinder. But if this—or any of the circulatory pipes—become blocked, pressure may build up in the system and serious problems arise.

Precautions against freezing

Insulation is your first line of defence against frost, and you should start by considering the garden.

Frost in the UK rarely penetrates more than 450mm below ground level. But to be absolutely sure they do not freeze, supply pipes should be buried between 820mm and 1000mm deep.

Make sure that your pipes are at this depth along their entire length and that garden landscaping does not reduce it. Most homes have an external, key-operated stopcock under a cover on the boundary of the property. If yours has one, check that it is operating properly and then wrap glass fibre roll around the tap to protect it. Remember that your stopcocks are the first things to tackle when a disaster occurs: they must be working properly (fig. 1).

Next check the point where the water supply enters the house. Common house renovation projects include installing damp-proof courses and excavating trenches around rooms below ground level. Make sure that you time this kind of work to avoid the worst of the winter cold and that you do not leave any pipework dangerously exposed overnight.

For a thorough lagging job you can use a length of split PVC drainpipe as insulation. Wrap glass fibre or jute lagging around the horizontal runs and then cover them with the pipe: deal with vertical runs by fitting the pipe around them and then filling the space in between with a loose-fill insulation such as polystyrene chips.

The roof space

UK houses usually have pipes and cold water storage cisterns in the roof space and, particularly if the loft is well insulated, these are prone to freezing in the winter.

Make sure, therefore, that all pipework

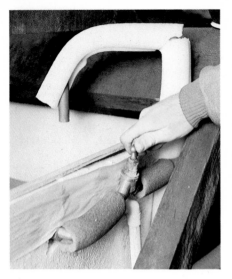

1 As well as insulating the cold water tank and pipework in the loft, thoroughly check the operation of the rising main stop valve nearby

2 Foam plastic insulation is an excellent protector for your pipework and is widely available in a variety of sizes and different thicknesses

5 However, before you actually cut the insulation to length, make sure that it does cover the entire length of the particular pipe which you are trying to protect and insulate

6 The next stage is to secure the insulation with tape at points where it could easily come adrift—such as at joints in the pipes or possibly at bends in the heating system

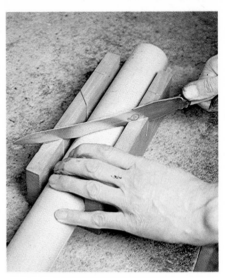

3 The insulation is easily split down its length for fitment, and adhesive on the split edges helps maintain a really good seal around the pipe

4 When lagging bends in a pipe, use a mitre box to cut mitred joints in the insulation. This then ensures a good fit between adjoining sections

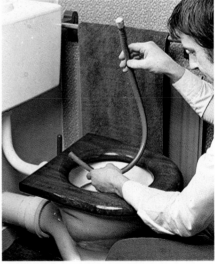

7 If you have no frost thermostat fitted on your heating system, set your boiler thermostat to 'low' and the timer to 'constant' when you leave the house during a frosty period

8 You can protect your WC by slipping the open end of a bunged rubber hose into the trap. If the water freezes, this will absorb the expansion that will inevitably take place

in the roof is completely lagged.

The cold water storage cistern and—if fitted—the expansion cistern serving the central heating system should be thoroughly insulated.

When insulating a cistern, make sure that the vent pipe can still discharge into it by fitting a large funnel through the top insulation.

Using lagging

Pipes can be lagged with either glass fibre blanket roll or purpose-made foam plastic pipe lagging. If you choose the blanket, wrap it horizontally around the pipe so that it covers the entire surface. Fix it in place with wire or twine tied round the pipe at intervals of about 500 mm.

Start lagging the pipes as close as possible to one end of the system and fix the lagging securely at this point (fig. 1). Run the lagging right up to the point where the pipe goes through a wall or through the floor and tie or tape it in place.

To insulate a cold water cistern, you can either buy a tailor-made kit, or adapt ordinary, blanket roll loft insulation material. In the latter case you must shape lengths of blanket to suit the positions of the cistern fittings.

Other precautions

Most heating systems incorporate a spring-loaded valve close to the boiler to guard against the possibility of an explosion. If steam even starts to seep out of this valve, you will know that the system is blocked and that you should shut down the boiler, open taps to let off pressure and locate the blockage.

Central heating systems can be fitted with a frost thermostat which raises the temperature of the building slightly if there is a threat of frost (fig. 7). If you do not have one, it is wise to keep the boiler on low all night in very cold weather.

Dealing with a burst pipe

Your first sign of trouble in the plumbing may be during a thaw when water starts

cascading from split pipes or dislodged fittings. This is what you should do:
● Immediately turn off the rising main stopcock, or, failing that, the key-operated stopcock outside.
● Open all the taps in the house.
● Turn the boiler to its lowest setting and do not draw off any more hot water.
● Locate the fault and try to rectify it.

Thawing out frozen pipework

If you wake up on a cold morning to find that water does not come from one of the taps, or that the boiler is overheating, the most likely cause is an ice plug somewhere in the pipework.

In this case, turn off the boiler (if it is overheating), and try to let off the pressure through the nearest hot tap or safety valve. Then, by a process of trial and error, locate the ice plug and thaw it out by one of the following methods—keeping a bowl handy in case the pipe has split.
● Wrap the pipe in a towel or rag which

rubber hose replacing
split section of pipe

hose clip

A. Emergency repairs. You can cut out a section of split pipe and replace it with a length of rubber hose (1). Alternatively, you can carefully cover the split with glass fibre paste, wrap on glass fibre

has been soaked in hot water.
● Wrap a half-filled hot water bottle round the pipe.
● Warm the pipe with a hair drier or fan heater.

Emergency repairs

The long-term cure for split pipes and damaged joints is to repair the joints and fit in new sections of pipework. This is easier where the pipe and joints are copper or plastic. However, lead joints must be *wiped*.

In modern systems fitted with compression joints, a freeze-up often forces the joints apart and does not burst the pipes. In this case, simply isolate the relevant pipe, unscrew the joint and re-assemble it with one or two turns of PTFE tape or a smear of jointing compound at the sealing points.

Otherwise, one of the emergency repairs described below will get you out of trouble. But do not rely on them for long.

● Isolate and cut out the damaged section of pipe, then bridge the gap with a length of hose held in place with Jubilee clips. If you cannot isolate the pipe effectively, ram two potatoes over the cut ends to prevent accidental leaks. Keep the rising main stopcock turned down to half pressure until a proper repair is completed.
● Sand the area around the damaged pipework, try to close the split by hammering it and temporarily mend the split with a two-part epoxy resin filler or proprietary pipe repair compound.
● Butter glass fibre filler paste around the crack, wrap it with glass fibre bandage, and then smear on more of the filler (fig. A).

In dire emergencies you can modify the bandage method by inserting a piece of wood—such as a matchstick—into the joint, rubbing thoroughly over the top of it with candlewax, and applying a tight bandage of the most waterproof material to hand.

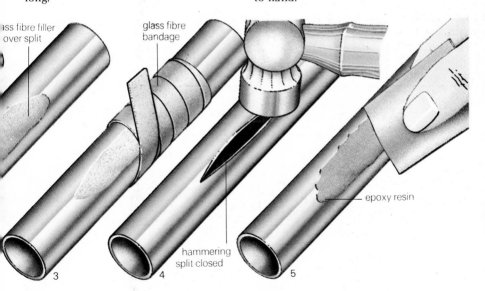

ass fibre filler over split

glass fibre bandage

hammering split closed

epoxy resin

3   4   5

bandage, then add more of the paste (2 and 3). Where the split is only a small one, hammer it together (4) and cover it with a two-part epoxy filler (5). Allow this to completely dry before restoring the water supply. Whatever repair you use, only open the main stopcock partway afterwards to cut down the mains pressure until a more permanent repair can be effected

Plumbing in a washing machine

Though an automatic washing machine is a boon to any household, many people are discouraged from buying one because it has to be plumbed in—both to the water supply and the drains. But providing you choose the site carefully and set about the work in a logical order, the job is not half as hard as it seems.

Note: In the UK, plumbing work is strictly controlled by local water authority by-laws. You must inform your water authority of your plans at least seven days before work starts. As well as giving practical advice, they will warn you against any possible infringement of their regulations. Work on the drainage system may need building regulations consent.

Choosing a site

Your first decision here is in which room to site the machine. In the UK, the choice is normally between the kitchen and bathroom, both of which have hot and cold water supplies and drainage outlets.

You have next to consider the type of machine, the space that will be needed around it, the existing layout of the room and the design and materials used in your plumbing system.

Of these, the plumbing system must inevitably take priority. It is no use choosing the ideal space-saving site only to find that you cannot then plumb in the machine without demolishing the house.

Drainage: In the UK, for a washing machine in a ground floor kitchen, the most suitable outlet for the discharge pipe is a back inlet gully, separated from the main discharge stack and connected to the main drain by a branch underground. This is often easier to

break into than the main stack and, as it is usually there to serve the kitchen sink discharge pipe, it is likely to be in the most convenient position already.

In older houses, the sink waste sometimes discharges over an open, trapped gully. You will probably be allowed to run the washing machine discharge pipe to here also, provided that the end of the pipe is below the grid.

If the pipe has to connect to the main stack, the latter will need a branch fitting. Though this is relatively easy to fit to a plastics stack, on the older, cast-iron or galvanized steel types the job is best left to an expert.

Water supply: Breaking into the hot and cold water supply generally presents less of a problem, as the final connections to the machine are usually made with flexible hose. Nevertheless, the supply must be near enough to the site to allow you to keep pipe runs as short—and as uncomplicated—as possible.

In the UK a cold-only supply might come direct from the rising main (usually the easiest arrangement if the machine is in a kitchen), though some water authorities do not allow this.

A hot and cold fill machine is best supplied via the cold water storage cistern or tank. In this case, as with some showers, low water pressure is sometimes a problem on upper floors or in flats and bungalows. Manufacturers generally specify a minimum 'head' of water—that is, the distance from the base of the storage tank to the point where the supply enters the back of the washing machine—and you should bear this is mind when choosing a site for your machine. If you cannot meet the minimum head requirement, consult both the manufacturer and your local water authority.

The pipe run must be arranged so that the branches do not cross one another, with the stop valves easily accessible. When you are planning the run, consider the best place to fit tee pieces to the supply pipes; it may be better to have a slightly longer run in order to avoid disturbing existing fixtures and fittings.

Breaking into the supply

Having chosen your supply pipes, turn off the nearest stop valves and completely drain the pipes by opening the taps at the end of them. With cistern-fed supplies, if there are no local valves, look for a cold supply stop valve on the pipe running out of the base of the storage tank and a hot supply valve on the cold supply pipe running into the base of the hot water cylinder.

If you still have no luck, you must tie up the ball valve on the storage tank and drain down the system. It is sensible to turn off the boiler or heat source before you turn off any water services. If you are taking the cold supply from the rising main, turn off at the mains.

To break into the supply, you must either cut out sections of pipe large enough to take tee fittings or remove and replace existing fittings. Opt for whichever gives the simpler pipe run.

Using the former method, measure and mark the cut sections very carefully against the tee fittings. Be sure to allow for the extra pipe taken up by the joints. If there is a joint already near a cut section, it may be easier to loosen this, make one cut and remove the pipe altogether (fig. 2). You can then trim it to the new length required on the bench. Make the cuts with a fine-toothed hacksaw, ensuring that the pipe ends are kept square.

Having prepared the pipe ends, fit the tee pieces.

Connecting to the machine

Somewhere between the tee pieces and the washing machine inlets, stop valves must be fitted so that the supply can be disconnected at any time. Some manufacturers provide these with their machines while others leave the choice of valve entirely up to you. Suitable fixing points for valves are normally the wall or the side of a unit.

1 When you find a suitable place to break into the supply, trace back along the pipes until you find the stop valves which will then isolate them

2 Having isolated and drained down the pipes, sever them with a fine-toothed hacksaw. Make sure you make the cuts as cleanly and as neatly as possible

27

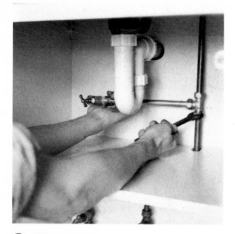

3 When you plan your new pipe run do not forget to include two extra stop valves so that you can isolate the actual supply to the machine. Then with careful planning, you can keep the run simple and the number of joints used to a minimum. Use compression or capillary joints to connect the piping

4 There are several different types of valve available and with certain types the flexible hose ends are easy to join as they can be simply screwed on, as pictured above. However, with the other types of valve available, different fixings, not always so easy to fit, will have to be used

7 Connection is then simply a matter of running the new discharge pipe down from the hole in the wall and jointing it up to the boss. Then solvent weld the joints only after you have assembled the pipes in a dry run and checked that the fall on the discharge pipe is really in the correct place

8 When the pipe run is jointed and in the right position, fit support brackets wherever necessary—either with masonry nails or plugs and screws. Back inside the house, you will need to connect the waste trap for the stand pipe at the point where the discharge pipe actually comes through the wall itself

5 The next essential task is to prepare the hole in the wall which is going to contain the discharge pipe. Make sure when you are chiselling out the hole in the wall that you make it large enough to accommodate any minor adjustments which you might find necessary to make as you go along

6 PVC drainage piping is easy to work with, but cutting it quickly blunts saw blades — it is better and more efficient to use either an old saw or medium-toothed hacksaw. Next, the discharge pipe should be connected to a stack with a spare branch outlet. The plug on the outlet is then opened up with a padsaw

9 The next stage of the plumbing work is to cut the stand pipe to the length you require and then to screw it to the trap and fit the necessary support bracket firmly to the wall. Now is the right time for you to check all along the pipe run for any noticeable leaks appearing at the junction of the joints

10 Finally, when you are quite happy that everything is functioning as it should, make good the hole in the wall with appropriate proprietary filler. Then roll the washing machine into place, being very careful that you do not tangle the flexible hoses or maybe compress them against the wall

Mark the points clearly then measure back and fit pipe runs—using 15mm copper tube in the UK—between these and the tee pieces. Where necessary, support with wall brackets every 1.2m. Fit the valve holders to the ends of the pipe runs before you fix them to the wall.

Finally, screw the valves provided into the holders and secure the flexible connections to the machine. On no account should you attempt to shorten the flexible fittings supplied with the machine: these are designed specially to length in order to balance out irregularities in the water flow.

If you are fitting your own valves, simply fit these to the ends of your pipe runs and connect them to the flexible hoses (figs 3 to 4). But as above, make sure that the valves are so positioned that the hoses do not cross or kink.

In both cases, test the pipework and all joints for leaks at this stage. If you find any, make repairs before going on.

Installing the discharge pipe

For the pipes themselves, follow the sizes and plastics type specified in the manufacturer's handbook. Most often these will be 32mm cPVC with solvent welded joints.

A. Below: A typical completed installation. Note that in some areas of the country taking the cold supply direct from the rising main is not allowed

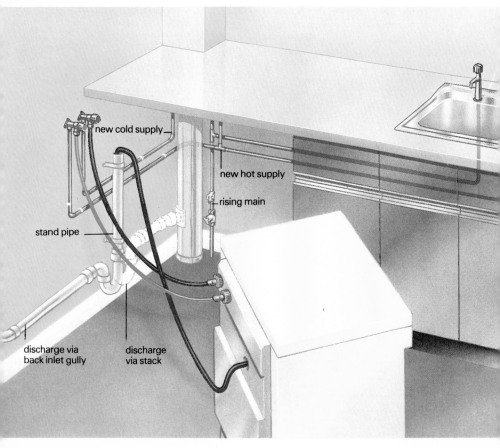

new cold supply

new hot supply

rising main

stand pipe

discharge via
back inlet gully

discharge
via stack

Connection to a back inlet gully: The simplest way to connect to a gully is to run the pipe just below the surface of the grid. To do this, replace the grid (if it is a metal one) with a plastic type, and cut a hole in it of the right size to take the pipe.

Alternatively, you may want to take this opportunity to replace an old gully (whether back inlet type or not) with a modern plastics back inlet gully. To do this, start by digging away the soil around the gully so that you expose the upper part. Remove the water in the trap beside it with a plunger.

Next, using a vitrified clay (V.C.) cutting tool, cut away enough of the pipe to accommodate your new PVC gully fitting. Bear in mind as you mark up for the cut that the new gully must finish above ground level and be far enough away from the wall to allow you to fit the discharge pipe (fig. A). Before you sever the pipe completely, support the gully from below to take the weight of the trap.

Remove the old gully and fittings above the cut completely. Using a V.C. chamfering tool, chamfer the remaining cut end to accept a flexible V.C.–uPVC connection. Afterwards, fit the new uPVC section and make sure that it is sited correctly in the gully trench and that the pipe is laid at a sufficient gradient to carry waste water away effectively.

You can now (at least temporarily) assemble the rest of the gully and fittings. Connecting the discharge pipe to the back inlet may call for a little trial-and-error. Start by connecting the bend and short length of pipe P1, adjusting the length of P1 so that P2 stands out from the wall the correct distance to accommodate pipe brackets. Then fit P3 and its bends, so that the fall of the pipe is between 18mm and 45mm per metre, and so that the lower bend is vertically over the bend connected to P1. Finally, cut and fix P2.

Now continue the pipe run through the wall following the same cutting and measuring sequence. Do not permanently solvent weld the joints until you have checked the run.

After the run has been fitted as far as the wall, fill in the space between the gully and the wall with a 1:3 mortar so that the concrete gully frame is held firmly in place. Finally, solvent weld the gully hopper joint and fill in the ground around the gully with earth.

Connection to a stack: Aim to run the discharge pipe to an existing branch outlet (fig. 7). If this does not have a spare outlet, then you can either fit a new multiple connector in this position, or a boss adaptor (of the type that can be fitted to an existing stack) to a length of plain stack pipe—whichever allows the discharge pipe to have sufficient fall. If you buy new components, make sure they are compatible with the existing ones—shapes and sizes vary slightly from brand to brand.

If you are connecting to an existing spare outlet, simply cut away the blanking plug and fit the new pipe in position. A boss adaptor is almost as easy to fit: consult manufacturer's instructions. A new connector is a little more tricky: the old connector will probably have to be sawn off, and the new one may not be big enough to bridge the gap. You might have enough 'slack' in the stack to take up the gap, or you may need to fit a slightly longer piece of stack pipe.

Final connection

At this stage, you should have run the discharge pipe through the wall and almost to the site of the machine. The final connection is made as shown in fig. A with a P-trap and stand pipe fitted to the discharge pipe length. The height of the stand pipe will be specified in the machine's handbook; in most cases, the outlet hose from the machine simply hooks into the top. This provides an anti-syphonage air break in the discharge piping.

Then connect up the washing machine and test it out. Watch carefully for signs of leaks in the discharge pipe especially where the outlet hose joins it.

Planning a shower

Taking a shower is the ideal way to freshen up, much more convenient than having a bath and considerably cheaper. Among the other benefits of a shower are its constant running temperature, and the possibility of fitting it away from the bathroom to avoid early-morning congestion.

You have the choice of converting existing room space to form an enclosure or of buying one of the many prefabricated enclosures now on the

or by laying on piping for an independent shower.

If it is difficult or impossible to lay on a suitable hot water supply, then an electric 'instantaneous' shower or gas heater may provide the answer, although both have disadvantages compared to a properly fitted shower. The instantaneous electric shower has a poor flow rate, and the gas shower needs ducting to the outside.

Note: You must inform your local water

market—many of which come complete with fixtures and fittings.

On the plumbing side, hot and cold water supply pipes have to be laid on as well as drainage, and these points go a long way towards influencing your choice of site.

Another alternative is to provide a shower over a bath, either by fitting combination bath/shower mixer taps

Above: A shower enclosure, and other simple washing facilities, can be easily incorporated in a conversion situated under the stairs

board of your plumbing plans at least seven days before the work starts. As well as giving practical advice, they will warn you against any possible infringement of their regulations.

The water supply

For proper operation of a shower, there must be sufficient water pressure at the shower rose. In many British houses, the water pressure at most taps (both hot and cold) is provided by a cold water storage cistern, mounted above the level of the water outlets. The higher the cistern above the outlet, the greater the pressure will be; the vertical distance measured from the bottom of the cistern to the outlet is called the *head*. For a shower, the head is measured to the rose and ideally should not be less than 1.5m, though in simple plumbing systems a head of 1m may be sufficient.

For heads of less than a metre, or where it is not possible to have short simple pipe runs, there are three main solutions. The first is to install a *flow booster*—a type of electrical pump which increases the pressure. Operation is automatic.

The second solution is to *increase the height* of the cold water storage cistern by raising it up on a sturdy wooden platform. Another solution is to use an *instantaneous shower* connected directly to the cold water mains.

In some areas of the UK, houses do not have cold water storage cisterns; instead, all cold taps and so on are supplied direct from the mains. Hot taps are usually supplied from a conventional hot water cylinder fed from its own small cistern.

With this arrangement it is not possible to fit a conventional mixer type shower: it would contravene water regulations. You can either fit an instantaneous shower or perhaps modify your plumbing so that the shower is fed from a suitable, conventional cold water storage cistern.

In Britain, a fully direct system like this will almost certainly use a 'multipoint' gas heater: you should consult both your gas board and your water authority about the possible problems of connecting a shower to such a supply.

Temperature fluctuations

Water starvation in either hot or cold supply pipes can cause temperature fluctuations in the shower, which could be annoying or even dangerous. It is very sensible to buy a shower that is thermostatically controlled, or at least has a temperature limiting device so that the water never gets dangerously hot.

Drainage considerations

Although deciding how to supply water to a shower can be tricky, it is usually possible to get over the problems one way or another. Leading the dirty water away, though, to a soil stack or waste water drain often presents far more constraints. PVC piping, being easy to work with, is the logical choice for this sort of job. But breaking through walling, both internal and external, is usually necessary if the discharge pipe is to remain completely hidden from view. And unlike hot and cold supply piping, the discharge branch cannot be taken under the floorboards unless the run is between, and almost parallel to, the joists underneath. The branch discharge pipe length is limited to a length of 3 metres and to a slope of between 1° and 5° (equivalent to a drop of between 18mm and 90mm per metre length).

An S trap can be employed if a pipe drop is required (fig. A), such as when underfloor drainage is possible, but otherwise a P trap is preferable. Use pipe of 42mm diameter.

If the shower base discharge pipe can be arranged to go directly through the wall and connection has to be made to an outside soil stack or waste hopper, much of the fall can be arranged externally.

Use professional help if you have to break into a cast-iron stack, though it is usually easier to replace the whole stack with the PVC equivalent so that the shower and any future additions to the system involve the minimum amount of work.

Installing a shower base

The first stage of the job is to prepare structural work—such as a timber frame for the enclosure—if this is necessary.

Thereafter the sequence is:

Run hot and cold water supply pipes to the point where a connection is made with the shower controller.

Use 15mm copper piping and T connections to connect with your existing hot and cold water pipes, keeping bends to a minimum and pipe runs as short as possible. Use either compression or capillary fittings—the latter are cheaper, and neater looking.

Remove the shower base (or tray) and its accessories from the protective wrapping, taking care not to scratch or damage these parts.

Lay the shower base on a protective groundsheet, and locate the tubular legs in the sockets welded on each side of the steel shower support frame. Fix the frame to the wooden shower support.

Secure each leg to its socket upstand using self-tapping screws.

Assemble the adjustable feet but hand tighten only as later adjustment is necessary. Place the shower base on its feet.

Fix the waste outlet to the shower base, incorporating the sealing washers

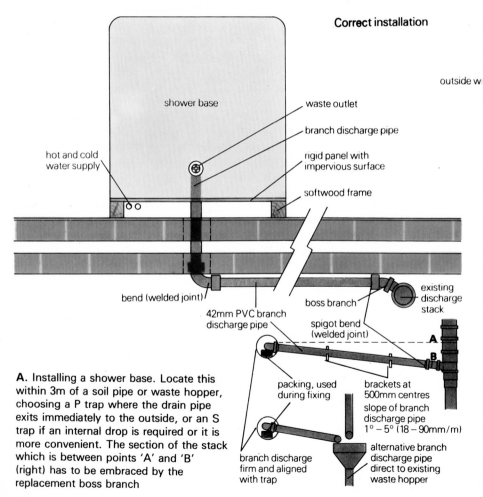

Correct installation

outside w

shower base

waste outlet

branch discharge pipe

hot and cold water supply

rigid panel with impervious surface

softwood frame

bend (welded joint)

42mm PVC branch discharge pipe

boss branch

spigot bend (welded joint)

existing discharge stack

A

B

A. Installing a shower base. Locate this within 3m of a soil pipe or waste hopper, choosing a P trap where the drain pipe exits immediately to the outside, or an S trap if an internal drop is required or it is more convenient. The section of the stack which is between points 'A' and 'B' (right) has to be embraced by the replacement boss branch

packing, used during fixing

branch discharge firm and aligned with trap

brackets at 500mm centres

slope of branch discharge pipe 1° – 5° (18 – 90mm/m)

alternative branch discharge pipe direct to existing waste hopper

34

provided and using a waterproof mastic to complete the seal. Use a holding spanner while tightening the larger nut with an adjustable spanner.

Attach a short length of pipe to the trap and temporarily secure the trap to the waste outlet, then mark on the wall the exit position of the pipe.

Cut a hole through the wall for the discharge pipe at this point.

Reposition the shower base, then using a bradawl mark the floor fixing points of its supporting board.

Check the level of the shower base,

ensuring that the trap has sufficient ground clearance, and tighten the fixing nut on each leg.

On solid floors it is difficult to drill and plug for eight screws and still have perfect alignment. It is easier to fix the support board on its own to the floor, attaching the feet later.

Temporarily link together the trap with a short length of pipe, arranged to protrude through the wall near to where it is to discharge into a hopper or stack.

If discharge is made to a soil stack, mark a point on the stack which is level with the protruding pipe and another point a little below this so that a drop of between 18 and 90mm per metre is obtained for satisfactory discharge.

Assemble a replacement triple socket, boss branch and pipe socket and then gauge the length of the piping which has to be removed from the stack in order to fit these. Transfer the measurement to the stack in such a way as to embrace points 'A' and 'B' (fig. A), with the pipe socket coinciding with the latter.

Cut out the stack length with a fine-toothed saw, taking precautions or using assistance to keep the upper and lower lengths in position afterwards.

Dismantle the triple socket from the boss branch and pipe socket. Push the triple socket into the top part of the stack as far as it will go. Then fix the boss branch and pipe branch on to the lower part of the stack. Complete the fitting by pushing the triple socket down into its final position.

Insert the spigot bend into the boss branch, attach brackets to the outside connecting length of the discharge pipe and fit this into the spigot bend. Twist the boss branch until the supporting brackets on the discharge pipe make contact with the wall.

The discharge pipe from the inside of the house should by now meet the discharge pipe attached to the stack, and the two can be marked for cutting so that you can fit a 45° bend where the inner pipe leaves the wall. Remove both pipes and cut these to final length.

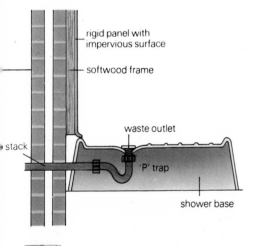

rigid panel with impervious surface

softwood frame

waste outlet

stack

'P' trap

shower base

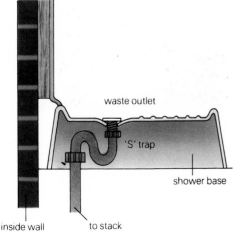

waste outlet

'S' trap

shower base

inside wall

to stack

Replace all pipes, the longer (outside) one with its fixing brackets in place. The shorter (inner) length is fixed first to the trap and then to the bend. Screw the trap to the waste outlet of the shower base.

Mark and fix supporting brackets, normally required only for the outside length.

Dismantle pipework and fittings that require solvent welded joints, prepare the joints and reassemble as before.

If the discharge pipe is to be led to an outside hopper, cut the protruding pipe length to fit a slow (45°) bend. Attach this to whatever length of pipe is necessary to complete the run at a convenient point above the hopper, and provide support brackets.

Make good the hole through the wall using a proprietary filler paste. There are now aerosol foam sprays on the market which are waterproof, allow for expansion or contraction, and are easier to work with than the more traditional compounds.

Test the pipework, first for stability and then for watertightness, using a pail of water until connection is made with the supply system.

Connection of the hot and cold water supply pipes to the shower controller (or regulator) is made in the course of assembling the shower enclosure. The valve and spray piping are attached to a mounting panel attached to the wall or set into the wall along with piping. With self-contained shower enclosures, the mounting panel is attached to the rear of the cubicle with a waterproof gasket arrangement.

Completing the enclosure

Once the shower base installation is complete, you can attend to the completion of the shower enclosure. This is a relatively simple job if you are using a prefabricated kit, which often requires little more than a few minutes with a screwdriver. Built-in enclosures requiring woodwork, tiling and other jobs take much longer to make but can be matched to the room.

Install an electric shower

An instant electric shower is an attractive proposition if use cannot be made of conventional hot and cold water supplies. In most instances, connection of the heater is direct to the mains water supply. The heater needs direct and permanent connection to the electricity supply through a double-pole linked switch—the cable from the heater unit connects to one side; cable leaving the other side connects the switch to the mains. The appliance must be earthed, and protected by a 30 amp fuse. For additional safety, site the heater well away from the direct spray at the shower.

You can interrupt the rising main at any convenient point. This Deltaflow unit requires a cold water supply which has a minimum static pressure of one bar which should be available from most mains supplies.

3 When you are fitting in the instant shower, you must make sure that you safely locate the double-pole linked switch on the other side of the wall to the actual shower unit. You must also ensure that it is connected up to the heater through the necessary hole in the wall

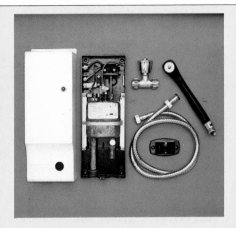

1 Installing an electric shower does require some plumbing and electrical skills so be very sure of your own abilities before you start work. Above is pictured the typical components of a shower kit which is readily available in the shops and DIY centres — the Deltaflow Showerpack instant electric shower heater

2 The first step is to remove the cover and mark the position of the fixing holes, and drill for fixings as required. Knock through for connecting wires. Cable entry to the heater is best made through the rear. Ensure this is correctly wired, tightening up the cable clamp firmly and securely afterwards

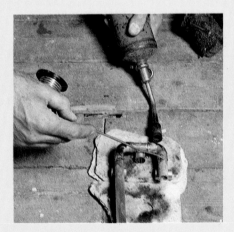

4 When making some pipe connections near to the shower heater, they should be tailor-made to fit the amount of space that is available to you in the unit. The best type of fittings to use are the capillary type up to the point that the heater fitting is used

5 The next part of the installing operation is to interrupt the cold water supply wherever is the most convenient point or junction in your supply. To do this you should use what is known as a T connector. If the pipe is in the loft you should lag it well

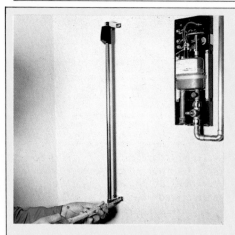

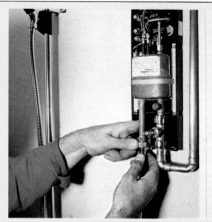

6 Now you need to go back to where the shower is going to be situated and mark the shower rail position. Then you should screw the rail firmly into place. However, before finally securing, make sure that you do not position the rail higher than the actual heater or the system will not work properly

7 Now you should connect up the shower's flexible hose to the water outlet of the heater unit. Then you should turn on the water at the mains and the flow tap. Next, you should carefully check all along the length of pipework for any leaks that are visible and that need correcting

8 Carefully repeat all the checking procedures done previously but now with the heater actually switched on. Where the water pressure is just too high, the restrictor may need careful and accurate adjusting to reduce the maximum flow of water which is being given out

9 When you have carefully done all the necessary checking tests and they have all been completed to your own satisfaction, you can finally set about replacing the shower unit cover. However, you should first make sure that you have connected up the two neon spade leads

Above-ground drainage

Above-ground drainage is an important part of any house. Understanding how it works enables you to clear blockages quickly and effectively and gives a useful insight into how future additions to your plumbing can be made.

Above-ground drainage systems are governed by a variety of regulations and local by-laws. Plans of all proposed alterations to your existing system must be submitted first to the building control department of your local council. The

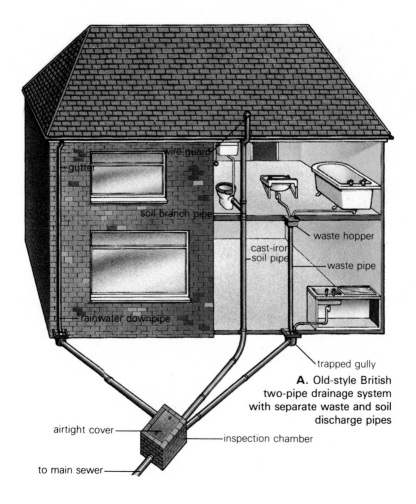

gutter

wire guard

soil branch pipe

waste hopper

cast-iron soil pipe

waste pipe

rainwater downpipe

trapped gully

A. Old-style British two-pipe drainage system with separate waste and soil discharge pipes

airtight cover

inspection chamber

to main sewer

39

inspector there will be able to authorize the plans and also give guidance and advice.

Three main types of above-ground drainage systems are in common use, although variations and modifications are frequently used.

In the *two-pipe system*, found in British homes built before the 1930s (fig. A) soil and waste discharges are piped separately to the ground drain. 'Soil' describes effluent from the WC; 'waste' describes water not contaminated by 'soil', including washwater. The two pipes may or may not be provided with some ventilation pipes to balance out

pressures in the system, depending on its particular size.

A variation of the two-pipe system is still occasionally used for bungalows, but seldom on two-storey houses as the amount of pipework is considered extravagant.

The hopper head used in this system for collecting bath and basin waste at each floor can become foul-smelling in hot weather, and its waste pipe blocked by dead leaves and suchlike at other times. This causes the hopper to overspill, leaving stains on the face wall of the building.

In the *one-pipe system* (fig. B), used in

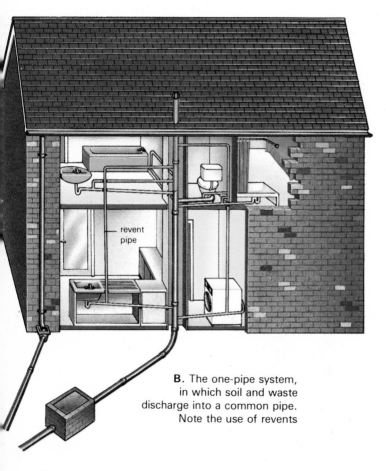

B. The one-pipe system, in which soil and waste discharge into a common pipe. Note the use of revents

revent pipe

back inlet gully

both Britain and North America, all the soil and waste water discharges into a single, common pipe which runs down an outside wall. Individual ventilating pipes from the discharge pipes, which carry the waste from the appliances, are all connected to a main ventilating pipe whose outlet is above roof level. In Britain, the one-pipe system can be seen on good-quality housing built between 1930 and 1950, but has since been superseded by the *single-stack* type of system (fig. C) for most forms of housing below five storeys.

Here, the soil and waste water discharges into a single pipe or *stack*,

built into the structure of the house. The top of the stack, which rises through the roof, normally provides the sole means of ventilation.

The efficient working of a single-stack system is dependent on all the branches being as short and as closely grouped on the stack as is at all possible.

Where a discharge pipe over the recommended length has to be installed, an extra vent pipe is run from the pipe near the appliance to a point at least one metre above the nearest entry to the stack. This balances out the pressures in the system which might otherwise result in the siphonage problems described below.

Because it is contained within the structure of the house, access to a single-stack system can often prove more difficult than to older systems. This is outweighed, however, by the saving on pipework and by the protection afforded against any damage caused by frost.

Sub-stacks and gullies

In single-storey houses, appliances are sometimes connected to a *sub-stack*—a short stack which runs directly to the ground drain and is ventilated independently of the main stack.

In many houses, waste water discharge from the kitchen sink runs to a separate gully (fig. A) which has its own waste trap (see below) and connection to the ground drain. In houses employing a two-pipe system, the gully will be below the hopper head. In single-stacked houses, the discharge pipe from the sink is connected below the gully grid but above the level of the water in the trap. This arrangement is commonly known as a *back inlet gully*.

Some local authorities permit other waste water appliances—such as washing machines and showers—to be discharged into the gully. The rules here are the same as those governing the sink discharge pipe.

Waste traps

To prevent foul air entering the home,

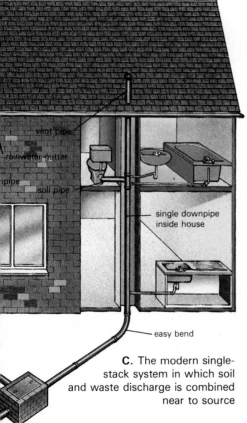

vent pipe

rainwater gutter

pipe   soil pipe

single downpipe
inside house

easy bend

C. The modern single-stack system in which soil and waste discharge is combined near to source

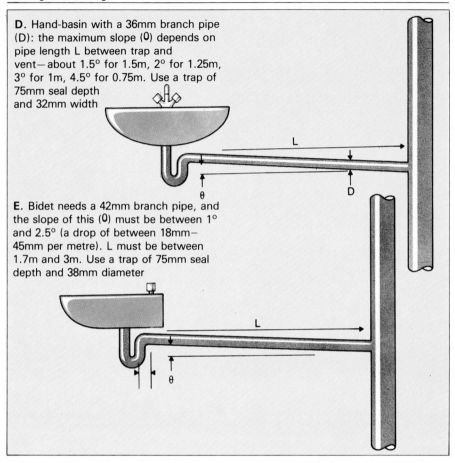

D. Hand-basin with a 36mm branch pipe (D): the maximum slope (θ) depends on pipe length L between trap and vent—about 1.5° for 1.5m, 2° for 1.25m, 3° for 1m, 4.5° for 0.75m. Use a trap of 75mm seal depth and 32mm width

E. Bidet needs a 42mm branch pipe, and the slope of this (θ) must be between 1° and 2.5° (a drop of between 18mm—45mm per metre). L must be between 1.7m and 3m. Use a trap of 75mm seal depth and 38mm diameter

simple devices known as *traps* are employed on each and every discharge pipe. A trap is little more than a depression or a bend which retains water but does not interfere with the flow of water through the pipe it serves. This *water seal* prevents air on the drain side of the bend from entering the room.

Traps come in a variety of shapes according to their function and fitting, and may in fact be incorporated within an appliance. P and S shaped traps are the most common, though they are now being superseded by the modern type of bottle trap. These are all used directly beneath the discharge outlet of baths, basins and sinks.

The water seal is the important part of the trap and the depth of water must be maintained. Loss of the trap through *self-siphonage*, *induced-siphonage* or *evaporation* can result in fumes or unwanted waste entering the house.

Self-siphonage occurs when a reduction of pressure occurs within the 'drain' part of a system, resulting in an individual appliance losing its seal when flushed or drained. Induced-siphonage occurs under similar conditions, but in this instance one appliance—such as a WC when flushed—sucks out the trap of another appliance where this trap is weaker or of incorrect depth.

Problems of evaporation may occur in

long hot spells if an appliance is left unused for any length of time. An outside appliance is particularly prone and the best thing that can be done to prevent the loss of water depth in the trap—hence weakening it—is to try to arrange for someone to flush the appliance from time to time.

In rare instances *blow-back (compression)* may occur when there is a burst of unusually high pressure in a system. A discharge high in the stack released shortly after another is nearing the bottom—and being slowed down by the bend there—causes the air between the two to become slightly compressed. Sometimes this pressure is sufficient to 'blow' the traps of lower waste appliances (bath, basin, bidet, sinks, shower) but not those of the WC.

Blow-back may also occur if discharge from one appliance (such as a WC) is allowed to force itself into a lesser discharge branch (such as that for a bath). This will occur if the centre lines of both discharge pipes meet at a common point—a mistake all too easily made when a person is considering making additions to a discharge stack.

Every type of trap has some form of access for clearing blockages. Older traps have a screw-in eye fitted to the lowest part. The newer, two-piece traps made of PVC are simply unscrewed if a blockage occurs. The access plate near to a WC is normally large enough to permit rodding in the event of any unexpected blockages.

Drainage requirements

The requirements governing above-ground drainage systems may seem unnecessarily complicated but failure to observe them can result in frequent blockages and the kind of siphonage problems described above.

In older houses, poor or haphazard installation of the various discharge pipes is often the most common cause of blockages.

Figures D and E show the design points to watch for when planning the drainage

Below: A plunger, ideally with a metal plate above the rubber cup, must be jerked vigorously up and down to create sufficient water pressure inside the trap to completely remove a blockage which has formed in the WC

Below: When trying to unblock a sink, try a plunger before attempting to dismantle a trap. Stuff a damp rag into the overflow—or use a suitable tape and bale out all but a small depth of water before you start using the plunger

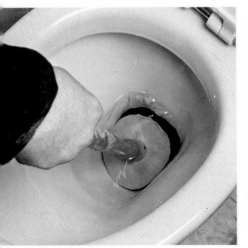

Above: Use an adjustable spanner or wrench to undo the eye in a metal P trap and gouge out the blockage using something like a screwdriver or a stick (above). Apply sealing compound before you replace the eye (right)

for a new appliance or checking on the efficiency of your existing system.

As a general rule, discharge pipes should be kept short and as free from bends as possible. Each must be connected independently to the relevant stack or pipe. In single-stack systems, the connections are best made as close together as possible.

Adding discharge pipes

When planning the run of a discharge pipe for a new appliance, bear in mind that it should follow the design recommendations in figs D and E as closely as possible—even if this restricts your choice of site.

Waste water discharges from two-pipe systems can usually run to the hopper head on the first floor, or to the gully on the ground.

Soil discharges present more of a problem as it is nearly impossible to break into old, cast-iron or earthenware soil pipes. Unless the branch fitting to the existing WC can be dismantled and replaced with a ready-made twin-branch fitting, it will generally prove easier to replace the entire soil pipe with one made of more workable PVC material.

Waste and soil discharge connections to a single stack are much more straightforward. Providing the site of the extra appliance is carefully chosen, and the run of the discharge pipe planned to join the stack close to an existing branch, then normally all you have to do is change this for a new fitting which has the extra discharge pipe socket you need. You could get this professionally fitted.

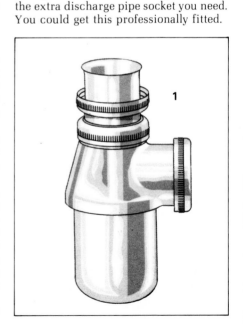

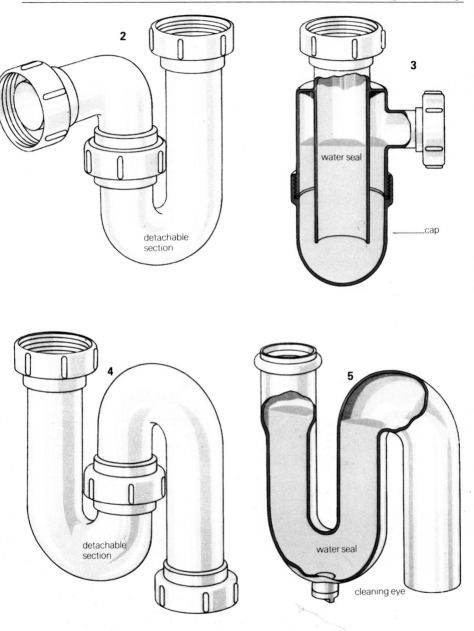

F. Left and Above: These are the different types of trap in common use in Britain today. These are fitted as close to the appliance as is possible. (1) Chrome bottle trap (2) Two-piece P trap of PVC (3) Modern bottle trap (4) Metal S trap showing seal and eye (5) Modern PVC, S trap

45

Dealing with damaged gullies

Domestic drainage systems consist of above-ground pipework from gutters, sinks, baths and WCs connected to below-ground systems of drains and sewers. There are variations in both above-ground and below-ground systems—but those of the above-ground system are probably more important when dealing with gullies. There are three main systems in use—the two-pipe system, found in British homes built before the 1930s; the one-pipe system used in Britain between about 1930 and 1950; and the single-stack system used on most modern British housing.

Note: You generally do not need

permission simply to repair drains, but check your exact situation with your local council before starting.

Gullies

Much above-ground pipework is connected directly to the below-ground system but in the UK—particularly for rainwater downpipes, waste water pipes in the two-pipe system, and ground-floor drains with the single-stack system—the connection is made by means of a gully. All gullies have a U-bend, which forms a permanent water seal, but otherwise, the designs can vary considerably.

Below: Replacing an old gully with a new one is a straightforward job, but often is hard work and causes disruption. For this reason alone, it is well worth maintaining your gullies and protecting them from blockages or damage

Modern gullies are designed so that the waste water enters the gully by a side or back inlet while at the top is an open grid for collecting rainwater and surface water from paved areas. Older gullies are not designed for back or side entry. They collect all waste water through the grid and are consequently more prone to overflow when waste matter lodges there.

In new UK properties, the building regulations insist that all waste outlets must be through sealed gullies. Open gullies are permitted only for rainwater discharge, though they can be used to replace similar types already in existence.

Gully blockages

Blockages are the most common drainage faults and an obvious sign is an overflowing gully or inspection chamber.

Test the nature and location of the blockage by lifting the manhole cover of the inspection chamber. If the chamber is clear, but the gully is overflowing, the blockage is in either the gully or the pipe between the two.

A blockage at the gully does not necessarily mean that the gully needs replacing. Remove the grid if it is obvious that accumulated debris is causing the problem, then scrape off the dirt and scrub it with a stiff brush.

If the grid is not blocked, it may be that the trap inside the gully is blocked by grease and sediment. Remove the grid and clear the deposits by scooping them out with an old ladle or a scoop made from a piece of tin nailed to a stick. Scrub the gully with hot water and washing soda, and rinse it thoroughly. To prevent future problems, make a removable bucket to collect the debris (fig. C) and empty it regularly. Some gullies already contain such a bucket.

Damaged gullies

The oldest types of gullies, made from concrete or glazed earthenware, are difficult to handle and are fragile; they have since been superseded by plastics gullies—first low-density polythene and then polypropylene—both of which share the advantages of low weight and compactness. However, plastics gullies must not be subject to large amounts of hot water or chemicals.

Frost is the most frequent cause of damage to pipes and gullies and it is worth checking up on this possibility after each cold spell. Permanent water seals often freeze and, in expanding, the ice causes the gullies to crack or splinter. When the ice melts, the debris joins the accumulating sediment and forms a blockage.

When frost is expected, you can guard against cracking by inserting a long, partially inflated balloon into the trap (fig. A), to take up the expansion of freezing water by collapsing. Empty the gully (see below) and feed the balloon through the U-bend by hand, making sure that the end is secured to the grid with string or wire.

Gullies and pipes are especially prone to damage if they are not laid or bedded properly. If the bed is insufficient for the loads above it (such as a drive), or the ground on which they are laid is unstable, the pipes may subside or crack and the joints between them become damaged. Flexible pipe joints and adaptors are now available for most of the different pipe materials and use of these makes the likelihood of such damage remote.

Run a standard drain test if you suspect that the pipework or gully is faulty. Lift the cover from the inspection chamber and insert a drainage stopper—available from plumbers' merchants—at the appropriate inlet channel. Insert a piece of hose around the U-bend to allow trapped air to escape, then fill the gully with water. If the water level drops appreciably within an hour, you have a fault worthy of investigation.

Digging out the gully

Unless the gully receives only rainwater, most of the plumbing facilities in the house, except for the WC, will be out of use for the duration of the work, so make arrangements for washing before you begin. For short distances, you may be able to connect the waste pipes directly to the inspection chamber using wide-bore hosing, thus maintaining your facilities.

Empty the gully by pumping a mop or rag up and down to push the water seal over the bend in the trap. Where possible, remove the waste-water pipes from the mouth of the gully and keep them aside.

The gully will be bedded in concrete and granular material which has to be removed and piled up during replacement, so clear the area around the gully as much as possible—preferably by at least 2m on all sides. Inspecting the depth of the drainage pipe inlets at the inspection chamber will give you some idea of the volume of soil and rubble that has to be excavated, but always overestimate the space you think is required. Plug the inlet hole with a drainage stopper.

Mark out digging lines around the gully with chalk or by scribing with the edge of your spade. Extend them at least 1m on each side of the gully and up to 2m in the direction of the drainage pipe.

Dig out the topsoil and set it clear to one side. Make separate piles of rubble and topsoil but leave yourself enough room to work in the trench, by not depositing excavated material within half a metre of the edge of the excavation. If, for any reason, you have to dig deeper than one metre, or if space is restricted, provide yourself with planking and strutting to shore up the trench and the piles of excavated material.

Remove all the loose material around the gully to a metre on each side, and expose the drainage pipe, up to a metre beyond the joint with the gully. Work carefully and methodically, and be careful not to strike the gully or any other parts of the drainage system—especially around the drainage pipe.

When they are exposed study how the gully and pipe have been bedded, and note the nature and position of the joint and the type of pipe which has been used. The joint requires special consideration, especially if this is where the fault lies. Sometimes the most common joint—

A. When the water in a gully trap freezes, the gully cracks and must be completely renewed. But the problem can be avoided by hanging a partially inflated balloon in it, as shown, to provide the necessary expansion room for the ice

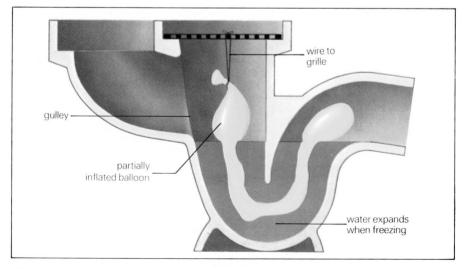

gulley

wire to grille

partially inflated balloon

water expands when freezing

1 To remove an old gully, start by pulling away the old iron grating. Then either use a plunger or piece of cloth fitted on a pole to empty out the existing trap of water

2 Now you can also renew old pipework above the grating with new uPVC pipes. Then carefully dig away the covering around the gully with a hammer and bolster

3 Continue until you have undercut sufficient material to insert a pickaxe blade. Use the pickaxe to smash the covering, working back towards the gully

4 Once the hole is big enough, use the hammer and bolster to chip away bedding material. You can then smash the old gully into removable sections

49

5 Work from the grating end back towards the point at which you will joint the new gully. Try to keep disturbance of the bedding to a minimum as you remove all the gully sections that are broken

6 Here, the vitrified clay drainage pipe is being completely severed with the use of a power saw fitted with a stone-cutting blade. This will then make a clean, neat cut behind the spigot which actually joins it to the existing old gully

9 Now the new gully is fitted in position, you must run a thorough drains test to check the joints for complete water tightness before you start filling in the hole

10 Next you should shovel in the bedding material, a layer at a time, making sure that every nook and cranny visible around the gully is well and truly filled in

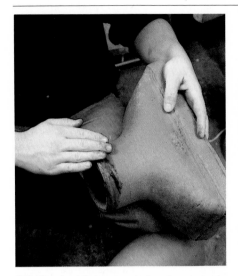

7 The bedding around the pipe end can then be cleared and the pipe stuffed with rag to keep debris out. Assemble the new gully at this stage, the one pictured is made of vitrified clay and uses joints of tar, gaskin and mortar

8 The new gully is joined to the pipe via a polypropylene sleeve. But first cut a new spigot to fit the pipe end. Fit it to the sleeve, position the gully on its bedding and join the spigot to the drainpipe with a mortar joint

11 Compress the bedding as you go, but take care not to disturb the gully itself. Bricks can be used to provide a side wall for the gully grating. Once in place you are ready to begin concreting

12 Smooth out the concrete to the edge of the grating. The final stage is to make good or renew any pipework around the gully. A good coat of paint will protect it from damage

sand and cement—is too rigid to allow settlement so that damage occurs if subsidence takes place.

Measure the dimensions of the existing gully, using a tape measure and calipers where necessary, and transfer them to paper; a standard gully has a 100mm diameter outlet connecting to a pipe of the same dimensions. Consider, too, whether the gradient of the drainage pipe affects the design as most standard gullies now have alternative designs suitable for drains with steep gradients. Based on these measurements, a builders' merchant can supply you with a suitable replacement.

The job of replacing a gully is of course much more straightforward if the replacement is a copy of the old. However, flexible joints enable you to fit modern-style gullies if these are preferred or more suitable, bearing in mind the old pipework.

Removing the gully

Remove the bedding material beneath and around the gully and pipework using a club hammer, bolster and cold chisel. When pipes, ducts, cables, mains and services are exposed, and their bedding is removed, support them temporarily with timber chocks.

Break the pipe with a hammer about 300mm from the joint, steadily striking in towards the gully until the pipe has separated all around its circumference. Then carefully tap the taped spigot until it separates from the drainpipe socket and remove the old gully. Wipe the socket clean, then stuff it with a rag to prevent fumes escaping and stop debris falling into the pipe.

In the case of a back inlet gully, remove the bedding beneath the gully so that you can move it downwards, away from the rainwater pipe. Then, in a series of twists and gentle pulls, separate the gully from the vertical pipe and remove it carefully.

Fitting the new gully

Remove the remaining concrete and screed until you have a solid bearing,

then tamp the ground to make the surface flat and firm. You must now make a timber former to receive the concrete which will form the new base for the gully. The minimum thickness of this base must be 150mm over a surface area of not less than 500mm × 500mm. Make up a dry concrete mix of one part cement to three and a half of 10mm all-in ballast and shovel this into the former. Place the gully in position immediately afterwards, working it gently into the concrete and simultaneously into the drainpipe socket and rainwater pipe. Remove or add concrete until the gully is in the correct position to meet all the connections. Use a spirit level across the mouth of the gully to establish its correct upright posture.

Joints to existing pipework

Until recently, the most common way of joining vitrified clay pipes with integral sockets for the joints was with sand and cement mortar. However, this method has the limitation of being inflexible.

To prevent such damage, bed the drain-

B. Below: Building a surround and cover stops the grating from getting blocked and also provides protection for the trap

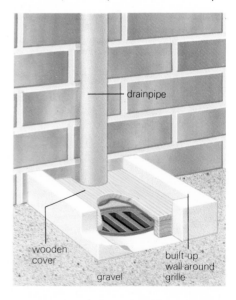

drainpipe

wooden cover

gravel

built-up wall around grille

pipes on either a granular bed consisting of one part coarse sand to two parts of 10mm ballast, or on a concrete bed of 100mm or 150mm thickness. Surround rigid pipes bedded in concrete with concrete to half-way up the pipe-barrel, then fill the trench 300mm above the top of the pipe with readily compactible material.

Cement-mortar joints can only be formed on pipes with connecting sockets already built for the purpose. Sockets should face the flow of the drain, with the spigot of the last pipe fitting into them.

Form a cement mortar joint by mixing one part cement to three parts fine sand, together with a little proprietary waterproofing agent. Wrap a piece of yarn, dipped in cement grout or tar, around the spigot of the gully (or pipe), place the spigot into the socket of the drainpipe and push it on as far as possible.

Caulk the yarn against the shoulder using a blunt chisel: this ensures that the spigot is centred evenly in the socket and prevents mortar from entering the pipe.

C. Below: A home-made bucket like this makes blockages easier to remove once they occur

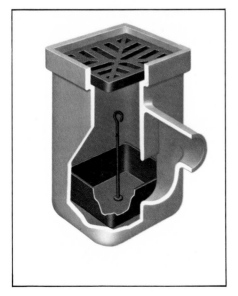

Pack the mortar into the space between spigot and socket with your fingers (wear rubber gloves) and finish the joint by trowel to an angle of about 60°.

Clay pipes with sockets can now be purchased with special polyester mouldings attached to them. Here, a rubber ring fits over the moulding on the spigot so that when it is pushed into the socket, the ring is compressed to form a watertight, yet flexible, seal.

Socketless, sleeved joints are an ideal method of dealing with clay or plastic pipes which do not have sockets. A polypropylene sleeve fits over the spigots of the butted pipes to form a flexible, watertight joint.

A new socket is then cut to make up the distance between the new gully and the drainpipe. The sleeve joins this to the gully pipe.

Each end of the sleeve contains a rubber ring which grips the walls of the pipes to form the joint. The two pipes are separated in the middle of the sleeve by a lip of polypropylene; this ensures that the two pipes do not bind against each other and that the joint therefore remains flexible.

Finishing off

When the gully is correctly positioned, and all joints have been completed, pack and tamp plenty of bedding around it and leave to dry.

Before filling in the trench, flush the gully with waste water and test the pipes and joints using the drain test.

When you are sure that the joints are watertight, remove any struts and timber left from the former. Fill in the trench to just below ground level with the rest of the excavated material, ramming it well down and removing any surplus.

Alternatively, fill the trench with medium gravel in 100mm layers, tamped well down, to a level of 100mm above the top surface of the pipe (150mm for flexible pipe). Then finish off the trench with all the previously excavated material and then lay a brand new covering of your choice.

Fixing a tap

Dripping taps can be a source of constant irritation for any household. Since the leak is usually caused by a worn-out or perished washer, one way of solving the problem is to replace the whole tap with a new one of the non-drip, washer-less type. A far cheaper way is to learn to mend the tap yourself.

Replacement parts cost only pennies and can usually be fitted in a few minutes, once you know how to take the tap apart.

How taps work

Most taps which have washers work in the same basic way: turning the handle raises or lowers a spindle with the rubber or nylon washer on the end in its seating. When the spindle is raised water flows through the seating and out of the spout; when it is lowered, the flow is cut off. But when the washer becomes worn and dis-

integrates, water can still creep through, irrespective of the position of the spindle. This is what usually causes the tap to drip. If the seals around the moving spindle are worn as well, leaks will also appear around the handle and the outer cover. Because you will have to dismantle the tap to replace either the washer or the seals, it is usually worth doing both jobs at the same time. If fitting new ones fails to cure the drips, the washer seating itself is probably worn. This is a common problem with older taps, and the cure is to regrind the tap seat.

Replacing a washer

To replace the washer on a conventional type of tap, start by turning off the water supply to the tap. Turn the tap on fully to drain away any water left in the pipe. Plug the basin, sink or bath to prevent any of the tap components slipping down the plug-hole.

The assembly which holds the tap washer and the spindle is known as the head. On older taps, it is covered by an outer shield which screws into the tap body. Newer taps have a combined shield and handle which must be removed as one unit.

To remove a conventional shield, make sure that the tap is turned fully on. Loosen the shield with a spanner or a wrench and unscrew it.

Modern shields/handles are either simply a push-fit on to the spindle or else are secured in place by a screw through the top.

If it stays fast, dig out the plastic cover in the top to expose the securing screw.

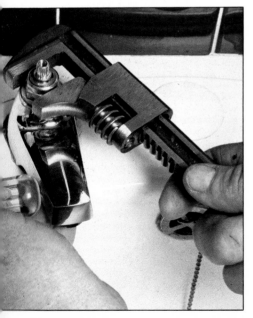

Left: A dripping tap can be extremely annoying for all concerned. But it can be easily corrected with the minimum of skill and expense

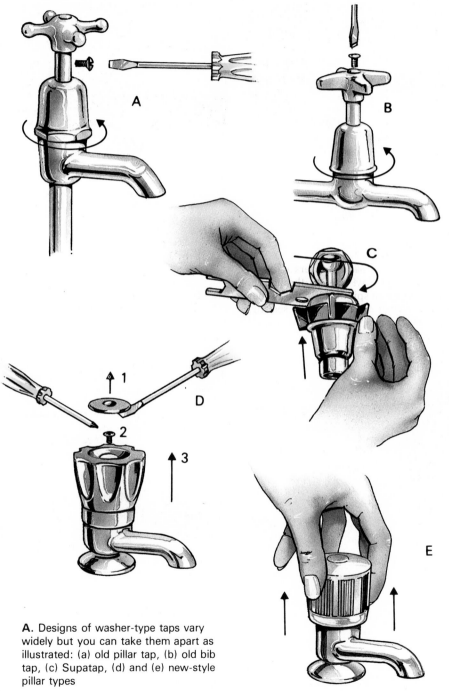

A. Designs of washer-type taps vary widely but you can take them apart as illustrated: (a) old pillar tap, (b) old bib tap, (c) Supatap, (d) and (e) new-style pillar types

1 On this type of tap, remove the cover to expose the securing screw. Completely undo this and pull the loosened handle upwards to expose the spindle. When you undo the locking nut, try to wedge the body of the tap against the nearest firm support to avoid putting any undue strain on the pipe

2 Unscrew the head assembly so that you can get at the washer. Check the seating in the tap body for corrosion while the tap is dismantled. On some types of tap, the washer is held to its jumper by a small securing nut on the base of the head—you will first need to carefully undo this with a pair of pliers

3 You can then manage to dig out the old washer and replace it with a new one. For a temporary repair you can actually reverse the old washer. To replace the spindle O-ring seals, you should dig out the circlip holding the spindle to the tap head. Take care not to damage the circlip

4 Once the circlip is loosened, you can slide the spindle out. You can then see the various O-rings used on this particular design of tap. If the seals are very worn, prise them off carefully with a pin. Slide on new ones and make sure these are properly seated before you start to reassemble the tap

With this removed, the handle can be pulled off (fig. 1).

The next stage is to remove the head. Locate the hexagon nut at the bottom of the assembly and loosen it, again using the wrench or spanner. Unscrew the head from the body of the tap and remove it. At the base, you can see the washer (or what remains of it) seated in its *jumper*.

On older taps the head assembly will be made of brass and the washer will be held in the jumper by a small nut. Loosen this with pliers, remove the old pieces of washer and put on the new one, maker's name against the jumper.

On newer taps, the entire head is made of nylon and the washer and jumper are combined in one replaceable unit which slots into the bottom of the assembly. To replace the washer, you simply pull out the old jumper and push in the new one.

Once you have fitted the new washer, you can re-assemble the tap and turn the water supply back on. If the new washer is seated correctly, there will be no drips from the nozzle and you should be able to turn the tap on and off with little effort.

Supataps

When replacing a washer in a Supatap, there is no need to turn off the water supply—this is done automatically by the check-valve inside the tap. To gain access to the washer, hold the handle in one hand while you loosen the gland nut above it with the other. Holding the gland nut and turning in an anticlockwise direction, unscrew the handle from the tap. As you do this, there will be a slight rush of water which will stop as soon as the handle is removed and the check-valve drops down.

Protruding from the dismantled handle, you will see the tip of the flow straightener. Push or knock this out on to a table and identify the push-in washer/jumper assembly at one end. Pull off the old washer/jumper and replace it with a new one. Before you re-assemble the tap it is a good idea to clean the flow straightener with a nail brush.

5 To replace a Supatap washer, start by loosening the locknut above the nozzle assembly. There is no actual need to turn off the water supply. The flow straightener can then be knocked out using light taps from a hammer. The washer and its jumper are situated at the other end of the tap

6 With the Supatap type of design, the washer is combined with the jumper and it needs to be carefully prised away from the flow straightener and then thrown away. A new washer—which must be exactly the same size to fit properly—can then be firmly and securely slotted into its place

Leaking spindles

If the leak is coming from around the spindle of the tap rather than the nozzle there are two possible causes. Either the O-ring seal around the spindle has worn out or else the gland nut which holds it is in need of adjustment.

To service the spindle, you have to remove the tap handle. On newer types of tap, this may have been done already in order to replace the washer, but on older cross-head taps the handle will still be in place.

The cross-head will be held on either by a grub screw in the side or by a screw through the top, possibly obscured by a plastic cover. Having undone the screw, you should be able to pull off the handle.

Once you have done this, mark the position of the gland nut at the top of the tap head against the head itself with a screwdriver. Next loosen the nut and unscrew it completely. Check the condition of the O-ring or packing around the seating below and, where necessary, replace it.

If the seal around the spindle appears to be in good condition, the leak is probably due to the gland nut above working loose. Replace the nut and tighten it gently so that it just passes the mark that you made against the head. Temporarily replace the handle and check that the tap can be easily turned. If it is too tight, slacken the gland nut. But if, with the water supply turned on, the tap instead continues to leak, then the gland nut will require further tightening to solve the problem.

Leaking swivel nozzles

Mixer taps with swivelling spouts are often prone to leaks around the base of the spout itself, caused by the seals in the base wearing out. Providing you are working on the spout alone, it will not be necessary to turn off the water. Start by loosening the shroud around the base, which will either screw on or else be secured by a small grub screw at the back.

Around the spout, inside the base, you will find a large circlip. Pinch this together with pliers and remove it, then pull out the spout.

Dig the worn seals out of the exposed base and discard them. Fit the new ones around the spout.

7 To cure a leaking nozzle, undo the shroud at the base—either by unscrewing or by releasing a screw. Pinch together the large circlip at the base. Use pliers for this but wrap cloth all around the nozzle so that you do not scratch the chrome surface

8 Then pull the spout from its seat and then dig out the worn seal in the exposed base. Place the replacement seal on the spout before refitting this. Replace the circlip and then firmly screw the shroud back on. Test the tap and check for leaks

Airlocks and water hammer

Rattling pipework, irregular and spluttering water flow from the taps and—occasionally—split pipes and joints are symptoms of two of the most common domestic plumbing faults: water hammer and airlocks.

Neither problem is serious if corrected quickly, and the work is not too difficult if you possess some plumbing skills. But if problems are ignored for any length of time, they are likely to worsen—and they can wreak havoc with other parts of the house if a pipe bursts or a joint starts to break up.

Note: In the UK, you must inform your water authority of your plans at least seven days before work starts. As well as giving practical advice, they will warn you against any possible infringement of their regulations.

Water hammer

This is a term used to describe any noise emitted by your pipework or water tanks. Identification is easy—you will notice the pipes rattling and vibrating as water flows through them, or else you will hear a succession of bangs and rattles whenever you turn a tap on or off.

The primary cause of water hammer is the water pressure of the mains supply. In areas where this is high, turning a tap on or off suddenly can produce a rapid build-up of hydraulic pressure in the water pipes—especially when the rate of flow through the pipes is quite high. The pipes then expand and contract under the increased pressure and the resulting vibration causes a shuddering noise that is amplified by pipes, tanks and other metalwork units.

The problem is made worse by insecure pipework which rattles against its supports, by faulty taps, or by a ball valve in a cold water storage tank that bounces on the ripples in the water (see below).

Curing water hammer

If your plumbing suffers from water hammer, do not immediately assume the worst: go about curing the problem in a logical manner, starting with slight adjustments to the mains water pressure.

Find the main stop valve—usually fitted under the sink in the kitchen—and adjust the setting so that the flow of water is slightly reduced. The cold water tap in the sink is usually supplied direct from the mains so turn this on and use it to check the flow rate. Very often a slight adjustment will cure the problem completely.

If this does not work, the pipework itself could be faulty. Check all the affected pipe runs for loose fittings and unsupported pipes. You may need to replace old bracket fittings with new plastic ones, but you could also fit soft rubber cushions between the pipes and the brackets to stop them vibrating.

Horizontal pipes need supporting every 1800mm or so along their length, though polyethylene or PVC pipes may need more frequent support—say, every 500mm or so. Vertical runs need less support as they tend not to sag, but you should make sure that they are secure and cannot vibrate.

In an indirect system, make sure the rising main is securely fixed to rafters and joists in the roof space—and not solely to the cistern. The pipe moves slightly as water passes through it, and if it is connected only to the cistern it may produce a low rumbling noise, especially if you have a galvanized cistern.

If this does not do the trick turn off the supply and remove the final 1m of copper piping. Replace this with a poly-ethylene or PVC pipe of the same internal diameter and connect it to the copper pipework and cistern using compression joint adaptors.

Taps

Leaking taps can often cause water hammer in the rising main or the distri-bution pipes from the storage cistern. More often than not the fault can be traced to a faulty gland in the tap body. The gland is a type of seal situated between the spindle and the washer which normally prevents water from leaking up the sides of the spindle. If the gland becomes worn or needs adjust-ment, water may leak through it when the tap is turned on and—more importantly—the spindle spins on and off very easily. When this happens, the sudden cessation of water flow through the tap can cause an abrupt expansion in the pipework and consequently some water hammer.

The first thing to try is tightening the gland nut. Put the sink plug in position to prevent your losing screws or nuts, and do not bother to turn off the water supply. Remove the tap handle and cover to expose the gland nut, then use an adjustable spanner to turn the nut slightly clockwise—but no more than half a turn. Replace the tap handle, then try to turn the tap on and off; re-adjust the gland nut if necessary until the tap can be turned without undue effort, but does not leak. Then reassemble the tap, applying petroleum jelly to the screw threads to protect them.

If readjustment of the gland is un-successful, you will have to repack it completely. Turn off the water supply and turn on the tap to empty the pipe before dismantling it. Remove all the nuts and washers above the gland nut and unscrew this to expose the packing around the spindle. Pick out all the

1 One cause of water hammer is broken clamps and fittings in the pipework. Check along all your pipes to look for these faults throughout the house. Where clamps and brackets have managed to spring loose, either replace them or refit them making sure that they hold the pipe tightly and securely in place

3 Any length of water piping which goes along horizontally for quite a distance will need some strong form of support at regular intervals. In the picture a notched length of timber, secured to the floor, has been used to support the rising main pipe which is situated in the roof space

2 Check that long unsupported pipe runs do not come into contact with any other fittings such as shelves, picture rails and ceiling joists. Support loose pipework with clamps or, alternatively, by squeezing small blocks of rubber between them and the fittings they are continually knocking against

4 Sometimes water hammer can be easily cured by just reducing the water pressure going through the water system. Go to the main stop valve, often under the sink in the kitchen, and turn it down slightly. This could well be enough to slow down the water flow and stop the irritating hammer

packing with a sharp instrument but take care not to scratch or damage the internal seating surfaces. Repack the gland using knitting wool steeped in petroleum jelly, packing it evenly round the spindle. Alternatively you can use an O ring seal bought from an ironmonger or plumbers' merchant. When you re-assemble the tap, adjust the gland nut as described above before fitting the tap cover.

Air chambers
Even with the mains pressure turned down, water hammer can still occur in almost any pipe connected direct to the mains. What is needed is some way to cushion the pressure shock wave created whenever a tap or ball valve is turned on and off.

The solution is to fit an *air chamber* on the offending pipe—a sealed tube containing air which evens out the changes in pressure. With the indirect type of system which is commonest in the UK, you may need an air chamber at the highest point of the rising main.

Air chambers can be bought ready-made, or you can make your own from a length of pipe—preferably larger in diameter than the pipe you are connecting it to. Fitting one usually requires nothing more than turning off the water supply, cutting the pipe at the appropriate place, and inserting a plumbing fitting (see figs 6 to 10). Then turn on the main supply: inflowing water will trap air in the chamber automatically.

Storage tanks
Water flowing into a cold water storage cistern (or tank) can cause ripples on the surface of the water already in the tank. This sets the ball float bouncing, rhythmically opening and closing the valve—and causing water hammer.

The easiest solution to this problem is to buy a purpose-made stabilizer to fit on to the arm of the float. The stabilizer is a plastic or metal disc attached to a short, adjustable arm which clips on to the float arm. The disc is adjusted so that it is sus-

5 A leaking tap gland is another potential cause of water hammer and can be easily identified. Remove the tap cover to check this out. Tightening the gland nut slightly may cure both the water hammer and the leak. If it does not, make sure that you replace the washer and repack the gland

6 An air chamber need be nothing more than a length of sealed pipe inserted, with a T-piece, into the rising main near to the water tank. Turn off the water at the mains and depress the ball valve so that you completely empty the pipework. Then cut through the rising main with a small hacksaw

9 Cut a length of copper pipe about 500mm long to fit into the third nozzle of the T-piece and so complete the assembly of the air chamber. Then seal the open end of the pipe with a brass top end, having first used plenty of proprietary sealing compound to make sure that the pipe is absolutely watertight

10 The next and final stage of work is to firmly secure the pipe to the T-piece section and then turn on the water supply at the mains again. This then actually traps air throughout the pipe. This final action completes all the preparation work that is necessary in creating an air chamber

7 Remove the cut end of the rising main from the cold water tank so that you can cut out the length of pipe required for the T-piece connection. Before using any compression or soldered joints, clean the cut edges of the pipe with a file to ensure that you get a really close, watertight fit

8 Fit the T-piece to the end of the rising main, using a proprietary sealing compound to ensure that the compression joints remain completely watertight. Firmly tighten the joint on the cold water tank and make sure that the T-piece is fixed at the correct angle before you actually secure this as well

11 However, you will still need to replace any lagging for the pipes that you may have removed in order to fit the air chamber. You will also need to carefully lag the new air chamber. Make sure that all the pipes are covered securely. The operation is then completely finished and the system ready to be used

12 Use a spirit level to check that all horizontal pipe runs slope down slightly from the water tank, so allowing air bubbles to rise. Air-cocks should actually be fitted in the same way as air chambers or stop valves. They can be opened with a small key to allow trapped air to escape

pended a few centimetres below the surface of the water and acts as a damper, preventing the float from bobbing quickly up and down.

If the ball is a metal one, you could, instead, solder a flat disc of copper to the underside, taking care not to puncture it. The disc should be about 100mm in diameter to be effective. As an alternative, temporary, measure you could hang a light colander below the actual ball assembly.

If none of these methods are effective, fit an equilibrium ball valve in place of the existing one. This is fitted in exactly the same way and is designed so that the water pressure on both sides of the piston valve is equal. The bouncing is thus damped out, although the ball is free to move up and down with the level of the water in the tank.

Pipework
One further cause of water hammer is faulty pipework. This can affect the water flow in two ways: a long, straight pipe run allows the rate of water flow to build up to the point where turning off a tap abruptly can cause a very sharp build up in pressure in the pipe. The second problem arises when hard water deposits in a pipe constrict the flow at some point. When this happens the speed of the water increases as it passes through the constriction, and falls again as it reaches a wider part of the pipe. This causes pressure changes along the pipe with the inevitable vibration and noise.

The cure for the first problem is to reduce the rate of flow slightly by re-routing the pipe so that it has a few bends in it which slow the water down. But when you are doing this, be careful not to create an inverted U-bend in the pipe which could encourage airlocks.

If hard water is the problem, you must drain the entire system and flush it with de-scaling agent. To discourage future scale build-up, you could suspend scale-inhibiting crystals in the cold storage tank or consider fitting a water-softening device.

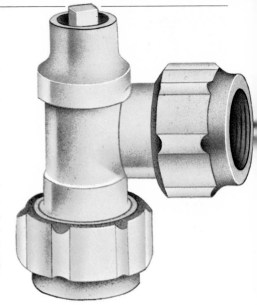

A. A typical example of an air-cock (**above**) and an equilibrium ball valve and air chamber which is found in a normal type of cistern (**right**)

Airlocks
An airlock is exactly what its name implies—a body of air trapped in a pipe between two volumes of water. When this happens the flow of water along that pipe becomes sporadic and irregular. In extreme cases the flow may be cut off altogether.

If you must drain the water system to allow yourself to work on it, take great care when you come to refill it. A common mistake is to try to fill the system too fast. If you have a direct water system where all the cold taps are supplied directly from the rising main turn down the main stop valve slightly so that the fast-flowing water does not trap air.

In the case of a more conventional indirect water system—where all the taps and appliances except the kitchen cold tap are supplied from the cold water tank —partially tie up the ball valve in the tank or turn down the stop valve on the pipe supplying it so that the tank fills slowly.

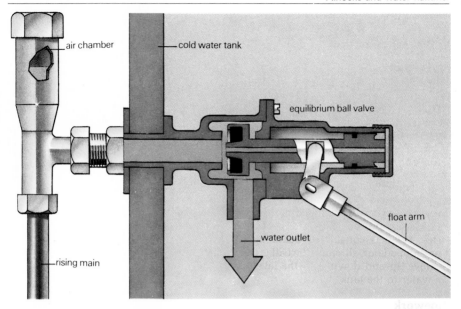

air chamber
cold water tank
equilibrium ball valve
float arm
water outlet
rising main

If after all this you still have an airlock in one of the pipes, you may be able to remove it using water pressure. Connect a length of hose between the kitchen cold tap (or any tap supplied directly from the main) and the tap on the end of the affected pipe. Secure the hose at each end with hose clips and turn both taps on for a couple of minutes. The pressure from the mains tap should blow the bubble out of the affected pipe and back up to either the water tank (if it is a cold water pipe) or the hot water cylinder vent pipe.

Another cure for persistent airlocks is to fit an air-cock at the highest point of the affected pipe. This is fitted in the same way as an ordinary stop valve.

Persistent airlocks indicate design faults and should be investigated carefully. The most common of these is the incorrect choice of pipe diameters for the various parts of the system. Pipe diameters must be closely matched to the appliances they supply and some appliances—such as baths and hot water cylinders—need a greater supply rate than others. The size of the pipe as well as the head of water determines the rate

at which water is supplied. Consequently small-bore pipes should never supply larger bore pipes and fittings because the smaller pipe would not be able to supply enough water to the larger one and air would enter to fill the spaces.

The exception to this rule is the rising main supply to the cold water tank: the diameter of the overflow from the tank should be greater than that of the main so that, in an emergency, water flows out of the tank faster than it is supplied.

One further cause of persistent airlocking is that so-called 'horizontal' pipe runs are indeed horizontal. 'Horizontal' pipes should, in fact, slope away slightly from the storage cistern or hot water cylinder so that air bubbles in the pipe get a chance to rise through the system while the water is stationary, and can eventually escape through the vent pipe.

If this is the problem with your plumbing you will have to drain the system and realign the pipes to allow the air to escape. Similar measures must be taken if you have very convoluted pipe runs where pockets of air can be formed. At the very worst, you may have to reroute the pipe run completely.

Cold water cisterns

In the indirect cold water systems widely used in the UK, most of the household water is distributed through a cold water storage tank or *cistern*. The main exceptions to this rule are taps for a garden water supply and a direct junction from the rising main to supply fresh drinking water, usually at the kitchen sink.

There are a number of advantages with this system. Firstly, it evens out the water demand loading for the water supply authority. In this way water is stored at off-peak times, such as overnight, and is then ready for instant use at times of maximum demand—such as between seven and nine in the morning.

Constant pressure is vital for both domestic hot water and central heating systems; and the lower-than-mains pressure helps to reduce stress in piping, as well as reducing the noise caused by the water flow.

Some modern cisterns combine hot and cold water storage in one but the majority of houses are still supplied from a single, large water cistern, usually

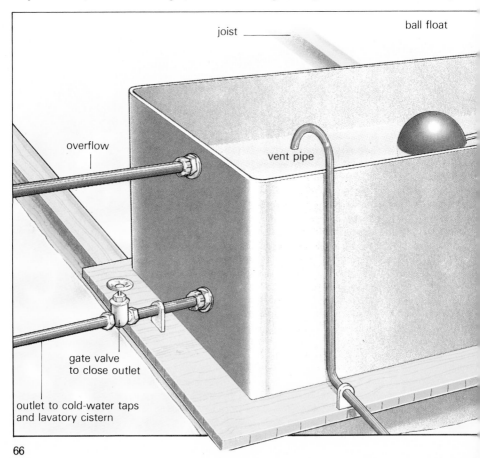

joist

ball float

overflow

vent pipe

gate valve
to close outlet

outlet to cold-water taps
and lavatory cistern

located somewhere in the roof space. Additionally, where an indirect system of hot water supply or central heating is installed, there is a smaller cistern to act as an expansion chamber and water supplier to the primary or sealed circuit.

In the case of a typical indirect water heating system, the heat exchanger coil within the water cylinder is supplied from this smaller expansion tank, while the water that is actually heated and used comes from the general cold water storage cistern (fig. 13). On no account

A. The main features of a normal cold water tank, with two outlets for cold water, an overflow pipe, a rising main, and a vent pipe which extends right from the hot water cylinder

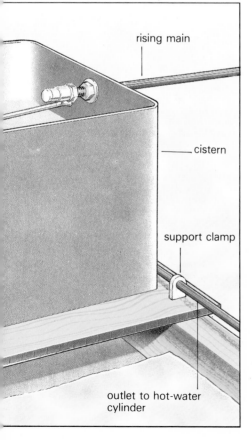

rising main

cistern

support clamp

outlet to hot-water cylinder

should an expansion tank be fed from a cold storage cistern; it should have its own supply direct from the rising main.

Your cisterns will house ball valves at the inputs from the rising main to keep the water inside at a constant level.

Usually there are two main outlets. One supplies cold water for the bathroom and is later branched to run to both taps and the WC cistern. This pipe should be 22mm in diameter at the cistern. The other outlet runs directly to the hot water cylinder. This pipe should also be at least 22mm in diameter but preferably it should be 28mm.

In modern installations both these pipes will be copper, and they should be fitted with gate valves so that either part of the system can be drained independently for repair. It is also a good idea to fit a stop valve to the inlet pipe from the rising main so that the whole sorted water system can be shut off for maintenance while still leaving a kitchen water supply.

Although electrically heated showers can be plumbed directly to the rising main as and where local regulations permit, mixer showers must take their cold water directly from the storage cistern. The reason for this is that a shower needs constant water pressure, otherwise there is a real danger of scalding when water is drawn somewhere else in the house. It is also essential to maintain equal pressure between hot and cold supplies. This is possible if both are pressurized by the same storage cistern, even though they may have independent supply pipes.

Shower outlets generally need a minimum head of water between the shower rose and the storage cistern of about 1m though this can be reduced to 900mm where the pipe run is very short and mainly straight.

Another vital piece of cistern pipework is the overflow pipe. This is fitted to the cistern approximately 25mm above the normal full water level and vents directly to the outside to prevent it from overflowing if the ball valve fails.

If your house water heating system

incorporates a hot water cylinder, either direct or indirect, the outlet of the vent pipe which rises up from the top of this will hang over the water storage cistern. Its purpose is to allow for the expansion of heated water, and to discharge any overflow caused by excessively high pressure in the hot water system (fig. 3).

A standard cistern filled with water weighs over 200kg and for this reason most cisterns are centrally installed in roof spaces.

Traditionally, cisterns were made from galvanized steel. These are heavy, subject to corrosion and are difficult to manoeuvre into the roof space. Consequently, they are increasingly being replaced by circular polyethylene cisterns which are light, corrosion free, and flexible enough to be squeezed through narrow trap-doors in the roof.

Cistern maintenance

All cisterns need to be dust and vermin proof (but not airtight) and insulated from winter frost. Whenever you take over a house you should make cistern inspection an early priority.

If the cistern is full of debris, it must be drained and cleaned. Make sure that all boilers and immersion heaters are switched off before you attempt this.

In most cases, draining is simply a matter of closing the stop valve on the cistern inlet pipe and then opening the cold taps around the house until the cistern reaches its maximum drain level —you will have to bale out the last few millimetres by hand. But in some older houses there will be no handy stop valve and you will either have to locate the rising main stopcock and turn off mains supply from here or tie the ball valve closed.

Once you have cleaned away all the debris in a galvanized cistern, search carefully for signs of corrosion. You can minimize future corrosion by suspending a 'sacrificial' anode of magnesium—available from plumbers' merchants—in the water. This should be connected to the tank rim by a short length of copper

1 In this installation the storage cistern is placed above the hot water cylinder, which helps to insulate it and prevent the pipes from freezing

wire or sheet. The magnesium will slowly dissolve away leaving the cistern walls relatively unscathed.

Non-toxic bituminous compounds manufactured specially for this purpose can be painted on new metal cisterns to protect them from corrosion.

Old metal cisterns can have their lives prolonged by this same treatment, but all traces of corrosion must be removed first. You can do this by vigorously attacking the surface with a wire brush and then rubbing down with wet and dry paper.

As you remove corroded layers, it is possible that small holes and cracks in the steel will be exposed. These can be effectively filled with epoxy resin adhesive or a glass fibre repair kit.

There may be borderline cases where you can temporarily patch holes using glass fibre filler and perforated metal sheet. And some clean holes can be repaired in the short term by drilling through the damage, then inserting a bolt

2 This galvanized steel water cistern has a corroded and dirty interior, consequently it is long overdue for replacement. Insulation around the tank is also a problem; polystyrene is an excellent insulator. It can easily be cut to fit around the pipes going to and from the cold water cistern

3 This is a properly insulated system with the cold water cistern, the expansion tank, and all the pipework properly protected. If the insulation is at all neglected to any of these areas, there could well be serious freezing problems during a very cold spell of weather during the winter months

4 To prevent the pipes from shaking and to protect the joints, you should firmly fix them to the roof joists with screw clips or suitable brackets. If you do not take these precautions you might well suffer from water hammer noises in the pipe system

5 Plastic cisterns must be laid on a flat but strong surface to prevent them collapsing under their own weight when filled up. Also, to ensure an adequate head of water for showers, the cistern should be raised even higher in the loft on a strong timber plinth

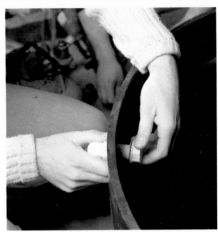

6 With the new cistern in place, carefully mark the positions of the various pipes leading to it at convenient points on the outside wall. Then you should make the necessary holes for the pipe connections using a power drill which is fitted with a suitably sized hole cutter attachment

7 A plastic screw connector is all that is required to secure the overflow pipe, but make sure that this is tightened up properly. If, for some reason, you cannot get a hole cutter to match the fittings exactly, enlarge the holes carefully with a file and clean up the raw and ragged edges

10 The outlets should be situated far enough above the bottom of the cistern to prevent any debris from getting into the pipes. Fit the outlet stop valves with compression joints and seal them with jointing compound. The arrow on the tap shows the flow direction

11 With all the fittings in place you can see how much easier it is to have them all on the same side of the cistern. If you decide to use soldered joints, remember the fire risk with plastics: do not solder immediately beside the cistern without adequate protection

8 One of the most important points to note with connecting pipework is to have a good seal on the fittings. Thoroughly coat the flanges on the interior sides of the outlet pipe connectors with proprietary mastic to ensure that you get a really good seal when you connect everything up

9 The next stage of work is to use compression joints to secure the outlet pipes to their actual fittings. You will need to make sure that the nuts are really screwed up tightly or you might well find, in the future, that the joints will leak and possibly cause some damage around the tank

12 The overflow pipe from the cistern should feed directly through to the outside. To save going to all the trouble of making up the necessary joints, you can just feed it straight through a small hole that you have drilled in the wooden plinth platform

13 The plumbing installation is now finally complete with only the necessary lagging and insulation to the cistern, overflow tank and piping to be fitted. Stop valves fitted on every outlet now make isolating the system much easier than ever before

with washers either side of the cistern wall. When tightened up this will provide a moderately watertight seal.

Once the repairs are made good, you must protect the cistern from further corrosion. Use at least two coats of the bituminous sealer, making sure that it is applied right up to the joints where outlet pipes leave the cistern. Leave the sealer to dry out thoroughly before refilling by opening the stop valve on the rising main.

If your cistern does not have a suitable cover, you should make or buy one.

Finally, check that the cistern and all its associated pipework are thoroughly lagged to prevent freezing. While it is rare for a cistern itself to freeze up, the ball valve nozzle—which stands out of water—is particularly vulnerable. If it should freeze, you can free it by wrapping a partially filled hot water bottle around the body of the valve for a few minutes.

For total winter protection, insulate the whole cistern—except the underside—with glass fibre lagging, loosefill chips contained within a hardboard frame, or specially designed fire-retardant polystyrene or strawboard lagging units.

At the same time, lag all other pipework in the roof space. Take care when you do this not to block the hot water vent pipe outlet which discharges into the cistern.

Ball valves
Your cistern might be fitted with any one of a number of ball valves, but the older types, where the float moves a washered piston inside a barrel, are more likely to be troublesome.

If you do have trouble with an old valve, cut off the water supply to it, then remove the float and arm by taking out the pin on which they pivot. If the valve is a 'Croydon' pattern, discharging downwards, the washered plug will simply fall out. But if the valve is a 'Portsmouth' pattern, discharging horizontally, you will need to unscrew the end retaining cap and then push the plug out

through its hole.

If a plug is sticking because of scale build-up, you can cure it simply by cleaning the plug with abrasive paper and then smearing it with petroleum jelly. To replace the washer, hold the body of the plug firmly in a vice and unscrew the retaining cap with pliers. If the retaining cap is stuck fast, you may have to pick out the old washer and force in a new one. Make sure the new washer lies flat in its seating.

If neither of these two repairs remedies the valve malfunction, it is probably time to fit a brand new valve.

Replacing an old cistern
Cut off the water supply to the old cistern and then completely drain it by running off water through the cold taps and baling out. Next, disconnect all the old pipe fittings and carefully lift out the old

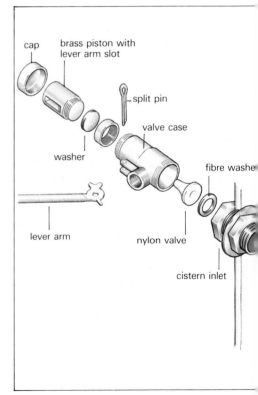

cap

brass piston with lever arm slot

split pin

valve case

washer

fibre washer

lever arm

nylon valve

cistern inlet

cistern system.

At all the removal stages lay down boards to distribute the weight of the cistern evenly over the joists and never step between them.

If your replacement cistern is exactly the same size as the old one, there will be little extra work involved in rerouting the pipework. Because of this, rectangular plastic cisterns reinforced with glass fibre are often more suitable for replacement work.

Although your old galvanized cistern may simply have rested across the joists, the new plastic one must stand on a flat base of 25mm board. Adequately support this with timber or it will buckle as soon as you fill it up.

It is far easier to cut the tapping holes in the new cistern before you manoeuvre it up into the roof space.

But if the trap door is too small to

accommodate the old cistern, you may find that only the drum shape polyethylene cisterns are sufficiently flexible to be squeezed into the roof space. In this case you must site the new cistern before rerouting existing pipework and marking the tapping holes.

Tapping holes in plastic can be cut either by heating up a suitable piece of copper pipe and burning the hole through, or by using a hole saw drill attachment.

The ball valve is fitted about 25mm down from the top edge of the cistern and most cisterns are reinforced at this point to bear the additional weight of the valve and its piping. Push the threaded tail through the appropriate hole and secure it on both sides with its locking nuts. Then connect the rising main to the valve using a compression joint which includes a special valve connector. If you do not have a stopcock fitted at this point, take the opportunity to fit one.

Special compression joint tank connectors, secured with locknuts, are attached to the cistern at each of the other tappings. Compression-joint the remaining pipework to these, rerouting or extending pipes where necessary.

Finally connect up the overflow pipe and ensure that the hot water vent pipe can discharge properly. Test the cistern in operation and secure any pipes subject to vibration with clips screwed to the joists before insulating the entire installation.

Insulation

When you have completed the installation it is essential to ensure that the tank and surrounding pipes are correctly insulated. All of the pipes, including the overflow and hot water vent pipe should be covered with thick lagging or pipe insulation.

Also make sure that the sides of the tank are insulated. Do not insulate the underside of the tank. Instead, lift the insulation from between the joists below so that warm air can rise and prevent the water in the tank from freezing.

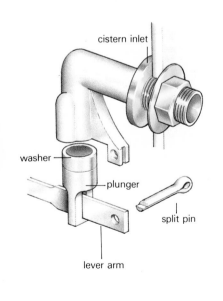

B. Exploded views of the Portsmouth (left) and Croydon (right) ball float valves, widely used today in the UK

cistern inlet

washer

plunger

split pin

lever arm

Renewing your guttering

However well they are maintained, old metal gutters and downpipes may eventually begin to show signs of decay. If the decay is far advanced, it is well worth considering replacing the system with PVC guttering.

PVC rainwater systems have several advantages over the various metal types. They do not corrode, nor do they require painting for protection—though they can be painted to suit colour schemes. Because PVC guttering is light, sections of it are easier to handle than their metal counterparts—an important consideration when you are working on a ladder. Being cheaper than cast-iron, PVC has virtually replaced it for home building and renovation in Britain.

Planning the new assembly

Sections of PVC guttering can be joined together in a variety of different ways. But with all types of half-round guttering, you fix the system to the exterior of the house in more or less the same way. The gutter sections are clipped into brackets screwed to the fascia boards beneath the eaves of the roof. The downpipes have wrap-around pipe clips which are screwed directly to the walls. Some other systems require no brackets for the gutters because they are screwed directly to the fascias.

Before you take down the existing guttering, measure it carefully to give you the lengths for the new gutters and pipes (fig. 1). Count and measure the stop-ends, outlets, shoes, swan necks and internal and external angles to work out the number and size of each part you will require.

When you are calculating the number

of support brackets and pipe clips needed, bear in mind that the existing system may not have been fitted with an adequate number. Gutter support brackets should be spaced no further than 1m apart, and pipe clips a maximum of 2m apart.

Removing cast or galvanized iron guttering

When you have bought all the replacement PVC components, you can start to dismantle the existing system. If your house adjoins another property, start at the joint nearest the dividing line between the two houses. If not, start at any convenient point along the run.

Remove the bolt holding the first joint together, using a junior hacksaw if necessary. Repeat the process for the joint at the other end of the length and then remove the section (fig. 3). When removing a long piece of guttering, take care not to let its weight catch you off balance while you are on the ladder.

When you have removed a section and taken it to the ground, unscrew the supporting brackets from the fascia board.

If you are dealing with Ogee-section guttering, either unscrew the fixing screws holding the lengths to the fascia board, or, if they are corroded, cut through them with a junior hacksaw.

Some cast-iron systems are supported by brackets which are screwed to the roof rafters. To gain access to the fixing screws on such brackets, you may have to remove the slate or tile immediately above it with a slate ripper.

When you come to dismantle a downpipe, start by removing the outlet section

Above: When you come to fix the downpipe of a PVC gutter system, firmly secure a plumbline with a nail or drawing pin to the fascia board immediately behind the outlet. This gives you a good guideline for positioning the pipe clips down the wall and fixing the pipe so that it runs vertically

at the top and, if fitted, the swan neck. You should be able to dislodge these by hand by pulling upwards, but if not, use a hammer to knock them from place (fig. 5). Remove the downpipe brackets by levering out the pipe nails with a claw hammer. Where necessary, hold an off-cut of timber against the wall so that you get more leverage.

Assembling the new system
Before you erect the new guttering, check that the fascia boards are in a sound condition.

1 Before you take down all the existing guttering, measure it carefully to give you the lengths for the new, substitute gutters and downpipes

2 The bolts holding the old gutter together may be badly corroded. In this case saw right through them using a junior hacksaw

5 You should be able to remove the swan neck of a downpipe by hand but if it is not possible, knock it out gently with a hammer

6 Before you start to assemble the new guttering, use a spirit level to check that all the fascia boards you are using are exactly horizontal

Scrape off any paint that has formed in ridges around the old guttering, then wash down the fascia and when dry apply primer to any bare wood. When this has dried, key the surface by rubbing it over with a medium grade of glass-

paper. Paint the boards with two under-coats and one top coat then leave them to dry out before erecting the new guttering.

Boards in particularly bad condition may have to be replaced altogether.

3 Lift the freed guttering out of its brackets and take it to the ground making sure that the heavy weight does not catch you off balance

4 If the fixing screws of a fascia bracket are too corroded to unscrew, then use a claw hammer to lever it completely away from the board

7 To assemble the system, begin by screwing the supporting fascia brackets firmly into place alongside the existing fascia board

8 When you are cutting a new piece of gutter to length, make a pencil mark on the underside of the section at the correct distance from the end

To assemble the system, begin by fixing the supporting brackets. Place one bracket at the top end of a run to correspond with the old one, and one at the bottom end in a similar position (fig. 7). Attach a length of string between the two brackets and make sure that it is taut. Check the string with a spirit level to make sure that it slopes towards the outlet position—the correct slope need be as little as 25mm in a 15m run—then use it as a guide for positioning the interven-

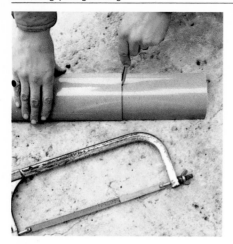

9 Fit a spare gutter section over the piece which is to be cut. Align its edge with the pencil mark and firmly draw the cutting line

10 Hold the length of guttering in place and cut through the line with a hacksaw. Then smooth down the cut edges with a medium file

13 When cutting a piece of downpipe to length, wrap a paper template around the pipe to make sure the cut edges are square

14 Mark and drill the pipe clip screw holes. In masonry walls, plug the holes with wall plugs, place a clip around the pipe, then screw it into place

ing brackets. It may be that you can fix all the new brackets in the positions of the old ones. But check constantly that both the spacings and the fall are correct.

When you come to an internal or external angle at the corners, hold the appropriate part in place and mark the

appropriate bracket positions: these vary according to the brand of system that you are installing.

When you have marked all the bracket positions, drill holes for the mounting screws into the fascia boards and screw each bracket home. With all the brackets

11 To join PVC guttering to an existing cast-iron system, clean the end of the iron piece, then apply some sealing compound to the area

12 Fix the special adaptor fitting into the end of the iron gutter and neatly clean off the underside with the point of a screwdriver

15 Working down the plumbline fix the downpipe sections to the wall. Remember to fit a pipe clip over every joint of the pipe

16 Finally, fit the shoe piece that lets into the drain or soakaway at the bottom of the pipe and attach the last clip to the wall

in place, you can start to position the guttering lengths within them.

Cutting and fitting

When you are cutting new gutter lengths, it is important to make sure that the cut ends are square. You can do this by fitting a spare section over the piece to be cut and using it as a template to draw the cutting line (fig. 9). Once you have sawn through a section, smooth the cut edges with a medium file.

Start fitting the guttering at the top end of a run. Clip the lengths into position in the brackets and join sections together.

Because PVC tends to expand and contract, even with quite small temperature variations, some systems make allowance for movement at each joint. In this case, the union clips holding sections together have marks on either side with which the ends of adjoining gutter sections are aligned. The resulting gap between sections allows for maximum expansion and contraction without weakening the new seal.

If you are faced with the problem of connecting the new guttering to a neighbour's iron system, special adaptor fittings are available for joining the two materials. Dry out and clean the end of the iron section, using a wire brush to remove any traces of rust. Apply sealing compound to the area then press the adaptor into place (fig. 12).

Fitting a downpipe

Unlike cast-iron systems, the swan necks for PVC guttering are not manufactured in one piece. Instead they are made up of an offset socket, an offset spigot and an offcut of pipe. The length of pipe determines the angle of the bend, thus giving you more flexibility in positioning the downpipe than you would have with cast-iron or galvanized metal.

To erect the downpipe, fix a plumbline with a nail or drawing pin to the fascia board behind the outlet. You can then use the string as a guideline down which to mark the pipe clip screw positions.

Place one of the clips around the bottom of the offset spigot, hold it temporarily in place on the wall, and mark its screw holes. Next, measure and cut the length of pipe to fit between the socket and spigot. To make sure that the cut end of the pipe is square, mark the length to be cut, then wrap a paper template around the pipe at the mark (fig. 13). Bore the holes for the pipe clip screws into the wall (fig. 14), plug the holes with wall plugs, then fit the swan neck in position.

Fit the downpipe down the wall, joining the sections according to the manufacturer's instructions, and fix a pipe clip at each joint to support the pipe. Finally, fit the shoe piece that lets into the drain or soakaway at the bottom of the pipe and attach the last clip (fig. 16).

Once the whole assembly has been fitted and joined, test the system by emptying a bucket of water into the gutter at the highest point of each run to check that there are no leaks.

Left: Make use of your rainwater by diverting it from a section of guttering into a storage barrel. These are readily available from garden centres

INDEX

The numbers in **bold** indicate detailed projects and the *italic* numbers refer to pictures.

Picture credits
Simon Butcher: 68, 69, 70, 71
Gavin Cochrane: 36, 37, 38
Ray Duns: 19, 20, 22, 23, 27, 28, 29, 60, 61, 62, 63, 80
Chris Fairclough: 49, 50, 51
James Johnson: 1, 75, 76, 77, 78, 79
Nigel Messett: 14, 15, 16, 43, 44, 54, 56, 57, 58
Gary Warren: 32

Artwork credits
Bernard Fallon: 9, 24/5, 39, 40, 41, 42, 66/7, 72/3
John Harwood: 2/3, 6
Trevor Lawrence: 55
Venner Artists: 10, 30, 44, 45, 52, 53
Gary Warren: 34/5